"Now that I've received Christ, what do I do?"

"The great adventure of the Christian life often begins with uncertain steps. Steven Pogue's book offers new believers clear biblical guidelines for those first steps and beyond. Here is challenge, encouragement, and best of all, preparation for the journey."

Dr. Reg Grant
Assistant Professor of Pastoral Ministries
Dallas Theological Seminary

"Steven Pogue offers us a book that explains the foundational truths of the Christian faith with simplicity, clarity and biblical depth. *The First Year of Your Christian Life* will get the new or just-beginning-to-grow believer off on the right foot in the Christian walk. This book is an excellent resource for the discipler or pastor assisting new believers in understanding how to begin to grow in their new relationship with Jesus."

Mark McCloskey
Director of Training, Campus Ministry
Campus Crusade for Christ

"People often ask me 'Now that I have received Christ as my Savior, what do I do?' *The First Year of Your Christian Life* gives the answers in a clear, biblical and practical manner. It takes the mystery out of the first steps of spiritual growth."

Dick Purnell
Director, Single Adult Resources

"When the foundation is well laid and firm, there is no limit to the height of the building. This book will equip you to lay that foundation. After that, the sky's the limit. I heartily recommend *The First Year of Your Christian Life*."

Dan Hayes
National Representative
Campus Crusade for Christ

"In my ministry with new believers in the business community, I find them asking the same questions that Steven Pogue answers so well in his book. I recommend it as a useful tool to help any new Christian who desires to be better grounded in his faith."

Paul W. Barger
Associate Director of Staff Development
Here's Life America

The First Year of Your Christian Life

STEVEN L. POGUE

First printing, March 1989
Second printing, June 1994
Third printing, April 2000

Published by
Campus Crusade for Christ
Integrated Resources
100 Lake Hart Drive
Orlando, FL 32832
1-800-729-4351

Library of Congress Cataloging-in-Publication Data
Pogue, Steve.
    The first year of your Christian life.
    1. Christian life —1960- . I. Title
    BV4501.2.P55545 1988   248.4   88-30066
    ISBN 1-57902-018-6 (previously 0-89840-195-X) (pbk.)
    Integrated Resources Product Number: 1525e
    1-800-729-4351

Unless otherwise indicated, Scripture quotations are from *The Living Bible,* © 1971 by Tyndale House Publishers, Wheaton, Illinois.

Scripture quotations designated NIV are from *The Holy Bible, New International Version,* © 1978 by the New York International Bible Society, published by the Zondervan Corporation, Grand Rapids, Michigan.

For More Information, Write:

L.I.F.E. — P.O. Box A399, Sydney South 2000, Australia
Campus Crusade for Christ of Canada — Box 300, Vancouver, B.C., V6C 2X3, Canada
Campus Crusade for Christ — Pearl Assurance House, 4 Temple Row, Birmingham, B2 5HG, England
Lay Institute for Evangelism — P.O. Box 8786, Auckland 3, New Zealand
Campus Crusade for Christ — P.O. Box 240, Colombo Court Post Office, Singapore 9117
Great Commission Movement of Nigeria — P.O. Box 500, Jos, Plateau State Nigeria, West Africa

To Sarah

CONTENTS

Chapter 1

The Journey Begins

*When someone becomes a Christian he becomes a
brand new person inside. He is not the same
any more. A new life has begun!*
(2 Corinthians 5:17)

In committing yourself to Jesus Christ, you have
made the most important and wonderful decision of your
life. And you're not alone!

Millions of Christians echo the statement of Senator
Mark Hatfield of Oregon: "Following Jesus Christ has been
an experience of increasing challenge, adventure and happiness. He is totally worthwhile. How true are His words:
'I am come that they might have life, and that they might
have it more abundantly.' "[1] Finally there is something in
life that is real, that lasts.

You've spent all of your previous life believing God
to be either nonexistent or irrelevant. Now you're learning
that He is very alive and extremely relevant. You may feel
like you've embarked on a journey and entered a new world.
You have!

This past year in Tacoma, Washington, a social

worker discovered an eight-year-old boy who had been con-
fined in a box for two years. His world was six feet long,
three feet wide and two feet high—the size of a coffin. He
had no windows, no friends, no books. He had been allowed
out of confinement only to use the bathroom and to attend
church. His stepgrandmother explained to police why she
kept him in a box: She feared he was mentally retarded.

The boy was placed in a foster home. A psychologist
found him to be socially deprived, but otherwise normal.
He asked the eight-year-old why he had never tried to escape. The boy replied that he didn't know of any different
life: He was amazed that other little boys did not grow up
in boxes.

You've been living in the box of life without God. It
seemed normal enough at the time. What else could there
be? You had friends and "toys." But now that Christ is in
your life, you'll be amazed at all the life you've been missing. There is a sense of wide-open spaces and freedom. That
old life wasn't any more than a coffin-shaped box that
meant spiritual death. Now you have new life.

You also have new questions. Perhaps you've been
wondering: Is Christianity too good to be true? What comes
next? Why don't I feel different?

You've experienced the first days of being a Christian—but what about the first year? It is like the dilemma
faced by the newlyweds who suddenly realize that marriage
involves more than a pretty ceremony. Relationships take
time and understanding to be cultivated.

This book is meant to help you in your relationship
with Jesus Christ. It is not a replacement for your Bible,
which really is your guidebook. And it won't replace the
valuable input you will receive from Christian friends and
a local church. But it will answer a lot of the questions you
probably have. I hope you will treat the pages ahead not as
chapters in a "How To" manual, but as visits with a fellow

traveler who is still learning about Christ and His love.

Total Love and Acceptance

You may have noticed the phrase "John 3:16" on stadium walls at NFL games or in the galleries at PGA tournaments. That refers to the most famous verse in the Bible: "For God loved the world so much that he gave his only Son so that anyone who believes in him shall not perish but have eternal life."

God has a unique kind of love for you. It is *unconditional* (not based upon meeting certain conditions). God took the initiative to care for you because He loves you. He does not love you based upon your performance. You don't have to do anything to cause God to love you. There is nothing you can do to cause God to love you any more than He already does—and there is nothing that will cause God to love you any less. He loves you, even more than you love yourself.

Until now you have probably only experienced conditional love. It's expressed in sentiments such as, "I'll love you for as long as you love me" or, "You'll always be my first love, unless I meet someone better for me." Conditional love is based upon what you do. Perform well on the job, on the team or in the relationship, and you are "loved."

In opening your life to Christ, you have found total love and acceptance. One new Christian told me: "Because of my past life [sexual abuse, physical abuse, drugs and several suicide attempts] I found it hard to believe that anyone could ever love me. This summer a friend showed me that she loved me even if no one else did, and she showed me that Christ loved me too. These past four months as a new Christian have been the best ones of my life."

God does not love you based upon your performance. That may be hard to comprehend if you've never felt totally loved and accepted by anyone. But it's true!

Unfortunately, you won't always feel like God loves you. There will be times when you find yourself doubting not only His love, but His existence. You'll feel like giving up. Don't.

When God gave you new life, it didn't come trimmed in lace and smelling of perfume. Jesus began His earthly life in a smelly, damp stable. He tasted real life, and that will be the flavor of your journey with Christ — no magic; just the promise of His presence with you.

Why I Can't Ski

The Christian life can be like snow skiing. I was introduced to the sport during my first winter after college. I stepped outside the ski lodge at Lutsen, Minnesota, into the windy blast of a sub-zero January morning. Icy Lake Superior lay only a few miles to the east. The air bit my lungs as I lumbered in boots and skis toward the chair lift.

Unfortunately, I slid onto the chair with another novice skier. He had no advice for my first ski run. Near the peak of the mountain I noticed a number of skiers springing off their chairs and falling onto other skiers. My partner suddenly jumped off. I remained seated in my chair, stubbornly convinced that there must be a saner means of exiting. There wasn't. In a moment I was riding the lift *down* the slope, trying to ignore the stares of other skiers.

I did manage to exit the lift correctly the second trip up the mountain. Pointing my skis down the mountain, I began skiing directly down the fall line, which became an appropriate description. It was a long and cold morning.

From the warmth of the ski lodge earlier that day, the slopes had looked inviting. I had watched skiers make quick cuts and jump moguls. It looked easy, but after my experience I realized it wasn't automatic. It took practice and instruction. Each successful skier had to resist quitting when he failed. I missed out on some great times because I quit trying to ski that day.

The Christian life is a bit like that. I have met people who have given up in their new relationship with Christ. They were told it would be easier, and because there wasn't anyone around to help them, no one to give them instructions, they quit. Maybe they had never really understood that God loves them. That He cares. That He hangs in there with us. That following Him, even in bad times, is part of the journey.

There's a Danish proverb: "The next mile is the only one a person really has to make." The knowledge that God loves you will keep you going when the next mile seems intolerably long: "For I am convinced that nothing can ever separate us from his love. Death can't and life can't. The angels won't, and all the powers of hell itself cannot keep God's love away. Our fears for today, our worries about tomorrow, or where we are—high above the sky, or in the deepest ocean—nothing will ever be able to separate us from the love of God demonstrated by our Lord Jesus Christ when he died for us" (Romans 8:38,39).

Theologian Karl Barth was reportedly asked one day in class to expound upon his greatest insight into Christianity. His students no doubt expected an extensive lecture on the sublime. Instead, Barth quoted from a hymn that has become a familiar children's song: "Jesus loves me; this I know, for the Bible tells me so."

That's not just a sentimental expression. As we'll see in the next chapter, it means something that lasts.

Growing Deeper...

(An opportunity for you to interact with the material in

each of the chapters.)

1. God says that He loves you totally and unconditionally. What does this mean to you to be so loved?

2. The reality of God's love becomes apparent as you get to know God through the Bible.* Read the first three chapters of John before you go to bed tonight. (John is the fourth book in the New Testament.) Underline verses that seem particularly important.

3. Memorize John 3:16. By memorizing it, you can carry it with you in your thoughts throughout the day and think about how much God loves you.

*Please Note

If you haven't purchased a Bible, do so! You may want to read chapter 6, "Welcome to the Bible"; it offers suggestions on what type of Bible to purchase.

Each book of the Bible is divided into chapters and verses, and appears as "BOOK   CHAPTER:VERSE." Thus "John 3:16" means "the Book of John, chapter 3, verse 16."

Recommended Reading

The Christian Adventure by Bill Bright (Here's Life Publishers). A Bible study booklet covering the basic beliefs of the Christian faith.

Chapter 2

Will It Last?

Your first year as a Christian.
What will it involve?

God intends for you to *enjoy* the Christian life, not just *endure* it. Yet, you may find yourself thinking, *All this is wonderful, but what if something happens? Will Christ leave me if I fail to act like a Christian or stop believing? Will it last?* You certainly aren't alone in asking those questions. It's better to face them now than hold them inside for years.

A white-haired gentleman cornered me one Sunday morning after I spoke at his church in Wawaka, Indiana. Wawaka is a tiny town on U. S. Highway 6, nestled between cornfields and Amish communities in northeastern Indiana. Religion, like many things in rural America, remains so private that I was a bit surprised to find someone asking me so earnestly about salvation.

"You sound as if you are certain of going to heaven," the man said. "That's something I've always wondered about." From his weathered face, his eyes looked intently into mine. His smile and quizzical expression betrayed his thought that there must be no final answer to his doubts.

"I used to wonder about that," I replied. "Christianity always seemed to be something you couldn't be certain of because it's all by faith. I remember asking Christ to come into my life and then wondering if He would leave."

I became a Christian during my sophomore year of high school. One Sunday morning in the fall of 1970, a group of medical students spoke to our youth group about God. But they didn't merely talk about God; they talked about Jesus Christ in personal terms, as if they had just finished having breakfast with Him.

I thought I already knew God. You couldn't get too excited about Him. I turned to God when I needed Him — whenever I was in trouble — and He always helped me out. God was like the vacuum cleaner I kept in the closet. Got a big mess? Pull out the vacuum and clean up the mess, then put it back in the closet until you need it again. It's very convenient.

Listening to those students, it occurred to me that what I had seen as a convenient relationship with God might not be a relationship at all. In fact, that attitude of "I'll look to God when I want His help" must be what the Bible calls sin. They explained that sin was not just breaking one of the Ten Commandments — it was an attitude of self-centeredness that included trying to use God. So I was still separated from God! My vacuum-cleaner religion wouldn't keep me out of hell.

Those medical students went on to explain that Jesus Christ had died for the sins of the whole world — including mine. Vacuum cleaners can't offer forgiveness, but Jesus does. My Hoover upright can't take away guilt, but Jesus can. It suddenly made sense that He had died to take away the barrier between myself and God.

I slipped into the empty church sanctuary after their presentation and received Christ. I asked Christ to forgive my sins, to come into my life and to change me. I was ready for something big to happen to me. I thought, *This must be what it's all about.*

But I felt no new sensations. There were no voices from heaven. Only the usual boring ride home in the family sedan that day to a perfectly ordinary Sunday afternoon. No high school cheerleaders fell in love with me that week. I was still too small for football and too short and too slow for basketball. The only things to greet me during that week were more Bs and Cs on my exams. And more zits.

I couldn't find anything out of the ordinary that entire week that I could attribute to God. I felt that I had become a Christian. But I wondered—my life had not changed immediately; and if my life had not changed, then perhaps Christ had not really come into my life or forgiven my sins. That was not the correct conclusion I should have drawn from my experience, but there was no one to tell me differently.

Perhaps you've come to Christ later in adulthood. You may wonder if God really cares about your family, your job, your financial problems. Will prayer and all this faith stuff make a difference?

Through my years of working with new believers in Jesus Christ, I have discovered that many Christians of all ages live with the same doubts and misconceptions. We not only begin our Christian life unsure about a lot of things, but we may also wander around for months or years before we discover any answers. Knowing where to go to find those answers will spare you the pain of a doubt-riddled faith.

Consider this statement:

> And what is it that God has said? That he has given us eternal life, and that this life is in his Son. So whoever has God's Son has life; whoever does not have his Son, does not have life. I have written this to you who believe in the Son of God so that you may know you have eternal life (1 John 5:11-13).

What is John, the biblical writer, telling you? Eternal life, and heaven, come with knowing Christ. It isn't something you merely hope to attain: John says "that you may *know* you have eternal life."

Eternal life is Christ's promise:

". . . whoever hears my Word and believes him who sent me has eternal life and will not be condemned; he has crossed over from death to life" (John 5:24, NIV).

"For My Father's will is that everyone who looks to the Son and believes in him shall have eternal life, and I will raise him up at the last day" (John 6:40, NIV).

Would Christ really promise eternal life and then not give it to you? Is it likely that Christ would try to deceive you? You can trust all of Christ's promises — including His promise of you being eternally united with Him both now and forever in heaven. Here is what the apostle Peter said about it: "And God has reserved for his children the priceless gift of eternal life; it is kept in heaven for you, pure and undefiled, beyond the reach of change and decay" (1 Peter 1:4).

There's a reservation in heaven with your name on it. It can't be misplaced, lost or erased. You won't get bumped because of overbooking. It is a priceless gift, guaranteed. Peter continues: "And God, in his mighty power, will make sure that you get there safely to receive it, because you are trusting him. It will be yours in that coming last day for all to see" (1 Peter 1:5).

But how can you *know* all this is really true?

A Matter of Faith

The Bible teaches: "And without faith it is impossible to please God, because anyone who comes to Him must believe that He exists and that He rewards those who earnestly seek him" (Hebrews 11:6, NIV). Faith is indispensable to the Christian life.

But what is faith? Is it just a feeling about God? A creed? A belief in what you know isn't true? There are a lot of misconceptions about faith. Let's evaluate three of the most common ones. We may understand what faith is if we know what faith is *not*.

Faith Denied

Bertrand Russell, philosopher and religious skeptic, was once asked what he would say if after his death he were to meet God and be queried about his unbelief. Russell replied: "I'd say, 'Not enough evidence, God! Not enough evidence!' "[1]

You may have a friend who scorns your faith by declaring, "I don't believe in anything I can't prove or see." But all of us live by faith. Your friend undoubtedly believes in his own existence and in his past, neither of which he can prove.

There *are* grounds for faith in Christ and, despite the denials by skeptics like Russell, there is plenty of evidence to consider. Lew Wallace set out to write a book disproving Christianity. Instead, he found evidence for Christianity convincing. He wrote *Ben Hur*, depicting the powerful love of the Christ he had come to embrace.

Attorney Frank Morison intended to write a book about Christ that would strip His life "of its overgrowth of primitive beliefs and dogmatic suppositions." But his study of the evidence for Christianity yielded an entirely different result. The first chapter of his book is titled "The Book That Refused To Be Written."[2]

Christianity rests upon history, not philosophy. The resurrection of Christ is an historical event. If Christ did not rise from the dead, then He is still dead, and all who trust in Him are fools. That's what the apostle Paul said (1 Corinthians 15:14-19). The evidence indicates that Christ *did* rise from the dead. Historian Thomas Arnold said he knew of no other event of history with better evidence than the resurrection of Christ. Books such as *The Resurrection Factor* by Josh McDowell and *He Walked Among Us* by Josh McDowell and Bill Wilson document the evidence for belief.

Faith Without Commitment

A second misconception of faith is to view it as intellectual knowledge devoid of personal involvement. People who hold this view know something of the content of faith but know nothing of its commitment. They may even be churchgoers who repeat their prayers by memory and know when to stand in the church service. But don't get in their way when they exit the parking lot! Their religion is shed on the granite steps.

To this one New Testament writer replies: "Are there still some among you who hold that 'only believing' is enough? Believing in one God? Well, remember that the demons believe this too — so strongly that they tremble in terror!" (James 2:19) The demons recognize God's existence, but they fail to submit to His rule over their lives. Awareness of truth without response to truth is not faith.

Faith Without Substance

Perhaps you have heard these statements before: "It doesn't matter what you believe in, as long as you believe" or, "If you want to believe in Jesus, that's fine with me. I've got my own beliefs." Both of these statements reflect a subjective view of faith. People are telling you that while Christianity is true for you, it isn't true for them because the subject (the person believing) outweighs the object (what is believed).

They approve not because they know your faith is true, but because they know you are sincere. Sincerity does not make a false belief into a true one! Increasing the intensity of one's faith doesn't make it any truer. The captain of the Titanic believed that his ship was unsinkable. Could he have saved the passengers by simply believing even more in his ship's invincibility? There's much more to faith than just sincerity.

What We Can Say About Faith

At this point you may be saying "Great! But what does all this have to do with my faith?" The previous misconceptions are all partly true because biblical faith involves elements of all three: Your faith has content (the objective); it involves commitment (the subjective); and there is risk (the speculative). By risk I mean choosing to believe without total proof: There is no final proof for the existence of God, just as there is no final proof for His nonexistence.

Faith is not a feeling divorced from reason. It is not mere knowledge of Christian doctrines. Faith is a choice. Remember your last commercial flight? You probably boarded the aircraft and traveled across the country without ever actually seeing the pilot. You assumed that the jet had a pilot and that the voice over the intercom was in fact his. You trusted him—even though he could not guarantee absolutely that the plane wouldn't crash. Traveling seemed a wise choice; you took it by faith.

Your faith will grow in proportion to your knowledge of God. Faith doesn't depend on the subject—you; faith rests upon the object—Jesus Christ. Your airplane flight wasn't successful because you believed in it; it succeeded because the aircraft was mechanically reliable and the pilot was able to take off, cruise and land safely. Your faith only enabled you to *experience* what was true.

When you experience doubts about your faith in Jesus Christ, you may conclude that people who are strong believers just choose to believe without any evidence. But healthy faith questions things and then *seeks an answer*. Doubts should drive you to the Bible to discover God's answers. D. L. Moody, a nineteenth-century evangelist who helped thousands find Christ, tells of his own discovery:

> I prayed for faith, and thought that some day faith would come down and strike me like lightning. But faith did not seem to come. One day I read in the tenth chapter of Romans, "Now faith comes by hearing, and hearing by the Word of God." I had closed my Bible and prayed for faith. I now opened my Bible and began to study, and faith has been growing ever since.[3]

Faith involves exercising trust as a response to what you know is true about God and His Word. Your faith will grow as you know who Jesus is and why He can be trusted. In the next chapter we will concentrate on the life of Jesus. Why is He so much greater than all other founders of world religions? Why is He so trustworthy?

Growing Deeper...

1. On a scale of 0 to 100 percent, how sure are you that if you died tonight you would go to heaven? Does it make sense now that you can be 100 percent sure that Christ will *never* leave you and that you will go to heaven?

2. Read John 20:24-31. Note Jesus' reaction to Thomas' doubts. Jesus does not condemn or ridicule Thomas for doubting. Instead, He presents him with the facts of His resurrection.

3. Read the third chapter of John's Gospel again. John always describes faith as active, using the verb *believe* rather than the noun *belief.* What specifically can you learn about faith in this chapter?

4. Memorize Hebrews 11:6: "And without faith it is impossible to please God, because anyone who comes to Him must believe that He exists and that He rewards those who earnestly seek Him" (NIV).

Recommended Reading

The Resurrection Factor by Josh McDowell (Here's Life Publishers). McDowell set out to disprove Christianity and in the process became a Christian. Here is the fruit of his research.

Know Why You Believe by Paul Little (InterVarsity Press). Answers questions about science, miracles, evil, Christ and world religions.

He Walked Among Us by Josh McDowell and Bill Wilson (Here's Life Publishers). McDowell and Wilson provide overwhelming evidence that Jesus *is* who the Bible says He was.

Mere Christianity by C. S. Lewis (Collier/MacMillan Publishers). Tightly reasoned defense of the Christian faith. A good book for the skeptical non-Christian as well.

Faith Is Not A Feeling by Ney Bailey (Here's Life Publishers). Through a warm narrative of personal experiences, Bailey concludes that faith often goes beyond our feelings and becomes a choice.

Chapter 3

Knowing Jesus

Yes, everything else is worthless when compared
with the priceless gain of knowing
Christ Jesus my Lord.
(Philippians 3:8)

Who is Jesus? You may be familiar with the Bible and be certain of His identity. Or you may feel like the student at Notre Dame who complained to me: "I have Christianity all figured out, but I just don't know how Jesus fits in with it."

Who is Jesus? He is called by a variety of names in the Bible: Son of God, Son of Man, Savior, King, Lamb, Judge, Word, Good Shepherd, Messiah. If you've committed your life to Christ, you have a relationship with Him. That's a great beginning! Developing that relationship involves getting to know Him better.

The best way to learn about Jesus is to read His claims concerning His identity in the Gospels. The Gospels are the first four books in the New Testament and tell the "good news" (which is what *gospel* means) of Jesus Christ. They were written in the first century A.D. and were based upon eyewitness accounts of Jesus' life.

Jesus was born about 4 or 5 B.C. (Our calendars are a little off.) The nation of Israel had been under foreign occupation almost continuously since the seventh century B.C., and the Jews fought to maintain national identity. Every faithful Jew kindled the hope that one day Messiah would appear and provide salvation for the nation by overthrowing Roman rule. *Messiah* is a Hebrew word meaning "the anointed one," and *Christ* is the Greek translation of that Hebrew word. *Christ* is a title, not Jesus' last name.

The bulk of the Gospel accounts is devoted to the three years that Jesus spent ministering around the Sea of Galilee in northern Israel. They tell us of the life and teachings of a unique person. Jesus, the Gospels explain, demonstrated His divine powers by healing the sick, blind and lame; by raising the dead; by walking on water and calming a storm at sea. His teaching lacked the exacting legalism and piousness that characterized so much of contemporary Judaism. He became tremendously popular among the masses in Galilee.

Throughout His ministry Jesus kept pointing the people to Himself. The masses wanted a political liberator. The religious establishment wanted their positions of power and piety recognized. Jesus pandered to neither group. Let's examine four incidents in the Gospel of John to determine what Jesus claimed about Himself.

Equal With God

In the Gospel of John, chapter 5, Jesus was accosted by Jewish religious leaders for healing an invalid on the Sabbath (the Jewish "Day of Rest"). They considered any expenditure of effort on that day a violation of God's command to maintain it as a day of rest. Over the centuries they had meticulously codified what was permissible, and Jesus' action flaunted their strict rules.

Jesus defended His action of healing on the Sabbath by explaining that God, as the sustainer of the universe, never rests but continually keeps working. And God is always doing good in human history. Since God cannot stop such working on the Sabbath, neither can Jesus stop His work:

> "My Father constantly does good, and I'm following his example." Then the Jewish leaders were all the more eager to kill him because in addition to disobeying their Sabbath laws, he had spoken of God as his Father, thereby making himself equal with God (John 5:17,18).

The Jews saw Jesus' claim to deity as a virulent blasphemy. During the centuries of occupation by foreign nations, many Jews had endured terrible sufferings to remain faithful to worship Jehovah, the one true God. How could Jesus, a good Jew, ever think of saying that He was equal with God?

Eternal Pre-existence

Three chapters later in John's Gospel, Jesus is conversing again with the Jewish leaders. He was in Jerusalem for the Feast of the Tabernacles, a celebration commemorating God's direction to Moses and the nation of Israel during their journey from Egypt to the Promised Land.

In this conversation Jesus made several claims. He said that He was the light of the world, that He could free men from sin and that anyone who believed in Him would not die. The Jewish leaders were again incensed by His seemingly preposterous claims but apparently decided to humor Him, hoping to reveal His inconsistencies. Not even Abraham, venerated founder of Judaism, had claimed to be immortal, so how could Jesus claim this? Jesus replied:

> "Your father Abraham rejoiced at the thought of seeing my day; he saw it and was glad."
> "You are not yet fifty years old," the Jews said to him, "and you have seen Abraham!"

> "I tell you the truth," Jesus answered, "before Abraham was born, I am!"
>
> At this, they picked up stones to stone him . . . (John 8:56-59, NIV).

His remarks were even more inflammatory because of His use of the words, *I am*. In the Old Testament, Moses saw a burning bush as he was tending sheep in the desert. Approaching the bush, God suddenly spoke to Moses and told him to return to Egypt and lead the Israelites out of bondage. God assured Moses that He would be with him.

Moses asked God who he should say sent him. God replied: "I am who I am. This is what you are to say to the Israelites: 'I AM has sent me to you' " (Exodus 3:14, NIV). *I AM* was not so much a label for God as it was an indication of God's complete ability to deliver the Israelites from bondage. Jesus ascribed this same name and power to Himself.

One With God

This third claim is recorded in the tenth chapter of John. It occurs at the Feast of Dedication, or Hanukkah. Jesus is again in Jerusalem, and there is considerable speculation among the crowds and religious leaders: Will Jesus announce that He is the Messiah? Tradition had always taught that the Messiah would be revealed at one such feast.

The Jewish leaders gathered around Jesus and asked Him if He was the Messiah. It may have been genuine curiosity, but more likely they intended to set a trap for Jesus, forcing Him to say something that would warrant His arrest and execution. Instead of giving them a direct answer, Jesus said that He had already told them who He was and that they had not believed Him:

> "My sheep recognize my voice, and I know them,

and they follow me . . . my Father has given them to me . . . I and the Father are one."

Then again, the Jewish leaders picked up stones to kill him.

Jesus said, "At God's direction I have done many a miracle to help the people. For which one are you killing me?"

They replied, "Not for any good work, but for blasphemy; you, a mere man, have declared yourself to be God" (John 10:27-33).

The Resurrection

Lazarus, a close friend of Jesus, became ill. He lived in Bethany, less than two miles to the east of Jerusalem. Jesus at the time was many miles further to the east, ministering along the Jordan River. After He heard of Lazarus' illness, Jesus waited two days before departing. By the time He arrived in Bethany, Lazarus was already dead and buried.

Martha, Lazarus' sister, went out to meet Jesus and exclaimed that her brother would still be alive if Jesus had arrived sooner. Then follows this exchange:

Jesus said to her, "Your brother will rise again."

Martha answered, "I know he will rise again in the resurrection at the last day."

Jesus said to her, "I am the resurrection and the life. He who believes in me will live, even though he dies; and whoever lives and believes in me will never die. Do you believe this?"

"Yes, Lord," she told him, "I believe that you are the Christ, the Son of God, who was to come into the world" (John 11:23-27, NIV).

Jesus moved near the cave-like tomb where Lazarus was buried. Praying aloud, He thanked His Father for hearing Him: "I knew that you always hear me, but I said this for the benefit of the people standing here, that they may believe that you sent me" (John 11:42, NIV). His prayer finished, Jesus commanded Lazarus to leave the tomb, and the dead man came out, still wrapped in grave clothes.

What These Claims to Deity Mean

Jesus made what seemed to be extravagant claims about Himself: equality and oneness with God, eternal pre-existence, and the source of everlasting life. These are not the statements of a mere mortal (at least a sane one). Jesus also declared that He had final authority over all the earth, that He would one day return and judge the earth, that He could forgive sin and that He was the only way to God. He said He could give life and fill man's greatest hunger. He called Himself the Son of Man, an Old Testament prophetic term for the Messiah. He allowed others to worship Him even though Jews were to worship God alone.

During the trial preceding the crucifixion, the Jewish leaders said this to the Roman governor Pilate: "We have a law, and according to that law he must die, because he claimed to be the Son of God" (John 19:7, NIV). Jesus of Nazareth was killed not for what He did, but for who He claimed to be. C. S. Lewis, the Cambridge literature professor who journeyed from skepticism to Christianity, once remarked:

> I am trying here to prevent anyone saying the really foolish thing that people often say about Him: "I'm ready to accept Jesus as a great moral teacher, but I don't accept His claim to be God." That is the one thing we must not say. A man who was merely a man and said the sort of things Jesus said would not be a great moral teacher. He would either be a lunatic — on a level with the man who says he is a poached egg — or else he would be the Devil of Hell. You must make your choice. Either this man was, and is, the Son of God: or else a madman or something worse.[1]

Christ is the unique personality of history. Of all the founders of major world religions, Christ alone claimed to be God! Abraham, Mohammed, Confucius, Buddha — none claimed to be God. Buddha, for example, told his disciples near the end of his life not to worry about remembering him, but to remember his teaching about the Way of enlightenment.

Each of these founders of world religions can be divorced from his teaching without a total and irreparable loss to that religion. But Christianity is built upon Christ: who He claimed to be and what He did. His teaching is almost embarrassingly self-centered. What else can be said of someone who declares: "I am the way and the truth and the life. No one comes to the Father except through me" (John 14:6, NIV)? But if Jesus' claims are true, then His statements are full of hope. We can know God because Jesus *is* God.

Fully God and Fully Man

Jesus Christ is not only fully God, but He is also fully man. He experienced hunger and thirst, loneliness, and the pain of betrayal and rejection. He suffered the humiliation of hanging naked upon the cross. He experienced temptations. He ate real food, cried real tears at the death of a friend and lost real blood during His crucifixion. Even His resurrection was physical. Jesus Christ was fully man.

What does it mean to us that Jesus Christ is fully God *and* fully man?

First, *because Jesus is God, He is worthy of our worship*. We should treat Him as God, with reverence and respect. The Doobie Brothers used to sing, "Jesus is just all right with me." But Jesus is more than just all right. He is not our buddy; He is our Lord.

The Lordship of Jesus means allowing Him control over every area of our life: not only our religious worship and our private devotions, but our job, our family, our finances, our attitudes. Knowing Christ should affect our relationships with others, how we pay our bills and what we watch on television. Giving Christ control of these areas isn't what gets us into heaven; giving Christ control is a response to our eternal relationship with Him. He is your powerful Lord. Love Him. Worship Him.

Second, *because Jesus is God, He is able to handle all of our problems.* There is nothing we face that God cannot overcome. Jesus is the "I AM" who can do all things. Jesus claims that He is able to make all things work for good in our life (Romans 8:28). In fact, He is "able to do immeasurably more than all we ask or imagine" (Ephesians 3:20, NIV). As you get to know Jesus better, I hope you will see that He has the power to do in your life what He promises.

Third, *because Jesus is God, He was able to reconcile us to God.* Jesus is more than a friend. He is our Savior. Until we understand this, we'll be like that college student who didn't understand how Jesus fit in with Christianity.

Fourth, *because Jesus is fully man, He is able to identify with all of our needs and problems.* There is nothing we go through that He cannot understand: "Because he himself suffered when he was tempted, he is able to help those who are being tempted" (Hebrews 2:18, NIV). By living among us, Jesus perfectly understood all that we feel.

Fifth, *Jesus' identity as fully man affirms our humanity.* We do not become more Christian by becoming less human. God created us in His image and wants us to enjoy life with all of its possibilities. He gave each of us talents and abilities that He wants us to develop.

This does not mean that following Christ will make you healthy and wealthy (though it will make you wise!).

There will be personal sacrifices. You may have to give up what is comfortable: an old lifestyle, private habits, a career path, financial success, even your life. But you will discover that in living as God intends, life will be purposeful even in great difficulties.

Now you know the answer to the question: "Who is Jesus?" But a second question remains unanswered: "Why did Jesus come to earth?" The answer to that question needs its own chapter!

Growing Deeper...

1. Think about the problems you are facing. Is Jesus able to deal with them? How does that affect the way you view these problems? Pray, thanking God that He knows your problems and that He will be there to help you through each of them.

2. Tell someone this week about your new commitment to Jesus Christ. There is something about making your commitment public that will help solidify it in your own mind. Read Romans 10:9,10 to find out why.

3. Read chapters 4 and 5 in the Gospel of John. Write out the impressions that each person or group of people has of Jesus' identity. Based on their impressions, how do they respond?

Recommended Reading

Jesus: A Biblical Defense of His Deity by Josh McDowell and Bart Larson (Here's Life Publishers). A fascinating and captivating study of the life and person of Jesus Christ.

The Uniqueness of Jesus by Bill Bright (Here's Life Publishers). A Bible study booklet covering the life, death and resurrection of Jesus Christ.

Chapter 4

Why Jesus Came

*You do not understand Christ
till you understand His cross.*
— *P. T. Forsyth*

You know a lot more now about Jesus' deity and humanity. If you've been reading the Gospel of John, you've seen Him heal a sick child and an invalid and offer eternal life. But do you know which event of His life Christ considered the most important? Look at what He told His disciples:

Now my soul is deeply troubled. Shall I pray, "Father, save me from what lies ahead"? But that is the very reason why I came! (John 12:27)

No one can kill me without my consent — I lay down my life voluntarily. For I have the right and power to lay it down when I want to and also the right and power to take it again (John 10:18).

For even I, the Messiah, am not here to be served, but to help others, and to give my life as a ransom for many (Mark 10:45).

Jesus appeared on earth, the Bible teaches, "that he might take away our sins" (1 John 3:5, NIV). That is why Jesus came. The focal point of both the Old and New Testaments is not the life of Christ, but the death of Christ. It was the *giving* of His life, not the *living* of His life, that dominated Christ's thinking as well.

When you understand what sin really is and what it means for Christ to be your Savior, you'll see why Christ's death is so vital to the Christian faith.

The Reality of Sin

If you ask someone what sin is, they usually reply, "Breaking the Ten Commandments," or they think of something extremely pleasurable but generally forbidden. But sin is far more than breaking one of the "Big Ten." Sin is an inner attitude: an inclination to rebel against God and His laws.

The Bible uses several words in the Old and New Testaments to describe sin: "err," "miss the mark," "transgress," "violate the law." Writer John R. W. Stott has observed that these words can be grouped into two categories. First, sin is shortcoming, a failure to hit the mark. The word was derived from an archery term used when the arrow would miss the target. This category of sin could mean a slip, blunder or inward disposition toward evil. The Bible explains in Romans 3:23, "Yes, all have sinned; all fall short of God's glorious ideal." Second, sin is a transgression. We *choose* to to sin, to break God's laws. First John 3:4 says, "Everyone who sins breaks the law; in fact, sin is lawlessness" (NIV).

Sin can be defined as a lack of conformity to God's character and laws. This means any attitude or action on our part that fails to be in accordance with all that God is.

God has a standard for morality: perfection. The Bible explains: "And the person who keeps every law of God, but makes one little slip, is just as guilty as the person who has broken every law there is" (James 2:10). People talk about keeping the Ten Commandments, but obeying them means having internal compliance as well as external. And we all fail there.

A standard of moral perfection makes us chafe, so we ignore God. It reminds me of Robert Frost's complaint against those who wrote poetry without poetic meter. Frost compared it to playing tennis without a net: The rankest amateur thinks he has the hang of it. Each of us wants to feel good about his own morality. We condemn others' faults while attributing our vices to environment or heredity. So you feel bad about what you did last weekend? Lower your net of moral standards. Feel guilty at how you've treated those people for years? Take the net down!

Pride keeps us from God. As C. S. Lewis puts it, "As long as you are proud you cannot know God. A proud man is always looking down on things and people: and, of course, as long as you are looking down, you cannot see something that is above you."[1] We are guilty of self-idolatry. We refuse to place God at the center of our life and prefer to worship our own desires, our own ideas of what is fair.

That is what the Bible means by sin. It doesn't necessarily refer to raping, pillaging or plundering. Those are sins, but sin at its most basic level is an attitude of wanting our own way over God's. And sin is universal.

The Consequence of Sin

God judges each of us for our sins and declares us guilty. The penalty is death: spiritual separation from God. The Bible calls it hell.

The concept of hell is nonsense to the people who see love as the totality of God. God wouldn't really judge anyone, would He? Isn't God a sort of senile and benevolent Grandfather in the sky who looks down at our sins, casts a knowing glance and excuses them as part of the human condition? Isn't God a God of love?

God is love, but love does not sum up God. It is an

attribute: Love is something that is true of God. Another attribute is His justice. God is also holy. He is without any imperfection or sin. He is morally excellent.

All of God's attributes are at work simultaneously. God does not suspend His justice or His holiness to show love any more than He would suspend His love to be just. His justice demands a penalty, and He has judged that penalty to be death: "For the wages of sin is death . . ." (Romans 6:23, NIV). What we earn for our sin, our "wages" as the Bible calls it, is death. By "death" the Bible means separation.

Some have erroneously concluded that the Old Testament God is full of wrath and the New Testament God is full of love. But God does not change. He shows love, mercy and justice in all ages. Jesus talked about love and about heaven, but He talked more about hell than He did about heaven!

Jesus explained: "Then I will turn to those on my left and say, 'Away with you, you cursed ones, into the eternal fire prepared for the devil and his demons' " (Matthew 25:41). He described hell as a place of torment, destruction and eternal punishment. Hell means living forever in anguish and pain – and without God.

It's horrifying. But we don't really understand the good news, the gospel, until we know the bad news about our sin:

> Once you were under God's curse, doomed forever for your sins. You went along with the crowd and were just like all the others, full of sin . . . . All of us used to be just as they are, our lives expressing the evil within us, doing every wicked thing that our passions or our evil thoughts might lead us into. We started out bad, being born with evil natures, and were under God's anger just like everyone else (Ephesians 2:1-3).

Jesus Our Savior

At the beginning of the chapter we talked about the death of Christ. Now you probably understand why Christ's death is so vital. Dante's *Inferno* depicts the entrance to hell as bearing this inscription: "All hope abandon, all ye who enter here." Hell would be the fate of all mankind without the death of Jesus.

Jesus' name in Hebrew means, "Jehovah is my helper or rescuer." An angel announced before the birth of Christ, "You shall name him Jesus (meaning 'Savior'), for he will save his people from their sins" (Matthew 1:21). John the Baptist, upon meeting Jesus, cried, "Look! There is the Lamb of God who takes away the world's sin!" (John 1:29) The word *savior* means "one that saves from danger or destruction." The book of Romans explains, "When we were utterly helpless with no way of escape, Christ came at just the right time and died for us sinners who had no use for him" (Romans 5:6).

On one occasion Jesus was teaching inside a home crowded with listeners. Some men brought their paralyzed friend to Jesus for healing. Unable to reach Jesus through the crowd, they resorted to removing tiles from the roof of the home and then lowered their friend to Jesus. All eyes were on Jesus, anticipating a miracle. But what He said was even more surprising: "Your sins are forgiven."

The Jewish leaders present immediately grasped the implications of Jesus' statement. "Who is this fellow who speaks blasphemy? Who can forgive sins but God alone?" (Luke 5:21b, NIV) Who indeed? Sin is primarily against God. It may affect many people, but sin offends God first and foremost. For anyone other than God to offer forgiveness of sin would be the height of blasphemy, for they would be presuming to be God.

Imagine that upon coming to visit you I drove my

car through your garage door. Stepping out of my car, I walk across the street and ask your neighbor for forgiveness. Your neighbor, who didn't like the color of your garage door anyway, grants me his forgiveness. I get back in my car and drive away, feeling quite forgiven. You make a mental note never to invite another author to your home, and you try to figure out how you can receive compensation for your damages.

If I have offended you by destroying part of your garage door, I need to ask you, not your neighbor, for forgiveness. So how can anyone other than God grant forgiveness of sin? They can't. But Jesus could, because He is God and man. Sin is against Jesus as God, and He as God can grant forgiveness.

There is another aspect to Christ's death and your forgiveness. Let's go back to that smashed garage door. This time I explain what happened and ask you for forgiveness. You say "I forgive you." But the garage door is still broken! Someone has to pay to fix it.

Although there's no such thing as a free lunch, *salvation* is free because someone else paid for it. You were saved, but not without a cost: "For God took the sinless Christ and poured into him our sins. Then, in exchange, he poured God's goodness into us!" (2 Corinthians 5:21) That is the meaning of *redemption*: You were bought with a price. The payment was Christ's death—His spiritual separation from God the Father—upon the cross.

What does that mean? As finite humans we can't really comprehend it. In Christ's death both God's love and God's justice are shown and satisfied. That is why Jesus' identity is so important. If Jesus were but another sinful man, He could not pay for humanity's sins; He would have to worry about His own sins. But if Jesus were God, then He could pay for what man owed. That is what you have placed your faith in. Francis Schaeffer explains:

True Christian faith rests on content . . . The true basis for faith is not the faith itself, but the work which Christ finished on the cross. My believing is not the basis for being saved — the basis is the work of Christ. Christian faith is turned outward to an objective person: "Believe on the Lord Jesus and you shall be saved" (Acts 16:31).[2]

The substitutionary death of Christ sets Christianity apart from all other world religions. Christians cherish a symbol, the cross, which would otherwise be an object of derision. Death by crucifixion was so heinous that Roman citizens were exempted from it for all crimes except treason. The Jews must have mocked those early Christians, whose naked leader had died such a humiliating and agonizing death.

Yet Christians think of the cross before the crown. It bought our freedom. One Puritan minister titled his sermon, "The Death of Death in the Death of Christ." The cross of Christ enables you to say, "I am sure of knowing God, and I am sure of going to heaven."

Life after death isn't a remote possibility; it is as certain as Christ's own resurrection. The Jesus who died for you is no longer dead. He is alive! His closest disciples proclaimed that. His enemies couldn't refute it. Jesus had risen. He conquered death, and those who have faith in Him need no longer fear it.

How secure is your faith? Eternally secured. But sometimes we may feel as though we've messed up in our new Christian life beyond what God could forgive. We feel guilty and far away from God. But that doesn't have to be the case! In the next chapter we're going to talk about the wonderful gift of God's forgiveness.

Growing Deeper...

1. The apostle Paul said, "Christ Jesus came into the world

to save sinners—and I was the greatest of them all" (1 Timothy 1:15). Yet Paul led a strict moral life as a Jewish religious leader. What does it mean to be a sinner?

2. How do you think God would feel if you looked to Him as "The Man upstairs" or "The Big Guy in the sky?" How does Christ's death for you affect the way you view your relationship with Him?

3. Read the Gospel of John, chapters 6 and 7. Why do the crowds follow Christ? Why do the disciples follow Christ? What is it that He wants His listeners to know about His identity?

Recommended Reading

More Than A Carpenter by Josh McDowell (Tyndale Publishers). McDowell deals with evidence for Christ, the Bible and Christianity.

Basic Christianity by John R. W. Stott (InterVarsity Press). Stott teaches about Christ's identity and His work on the cross for man's sin.

Chapter 5

When You Fall

What happiness for those whose
guilt has been forgiven!
(Psalm 32:1)

The Internal Revenue Service received this anonymous letter several years ago:

Gentlemen:

Enclosed you will find a cashier's check for $150. I cheated on my income tax return last year and have not been able to sleep ever since. If I still have trouble sleeping I will send you the rest.[1]

Each of us wants to feel forgiven for the wrong things we have done. The question is, where does this forgiveness come from?

As a Christian, all of your sins are forgiven. You probably believe that from the Bible. But how do you respond to it? A friend who counsels many believers commented: "Some Christians don't really believe they have sinned; others don't believe they are forgiven."

I would like to use our time together in this chapter to help you appreciate both the reality of your sin and the reality of Christ's forgiveness.

41

What Sin Is

Ernest Hemingway once remarked that what is moral is what you feel good after and what is immoral is what you feel bad after. That's a popular view of sin — many have lived by it. But it is not a biblical view. Biblically, sin is an attitude of wanting your way instead of God's way.

How much does sin matter to God? He cannot tolerate it. "Your eyes are too pure to look on evil; you cannot tolerate wrong," says the Old Testament prophet Habakkuk (Habakkuk 1:13a, NIV). "God is light; in Him there is no darkness at all," John wrote in his first New Testament epistle (1 John 1:5a, NIV).

That may seem unimportant. Hasn't Jesus paid for all your sins? Why be concerned about sin when God loves you and offers a wonderful plan for your life? Perhaps you should view sins as mistakes, mere miscues in life.

God never views sin as such. Because of one sin, Adam and Eve were exiled from paradise. Because of sin God brought a flood upon the earth's inhabitants in the days of Noah. He brought fire upon the cities of Sodom and Gomorrah because of their blatant immorality. Sin kept the original children of Israel in the wilderness for forty years. It kept Moses from entering the Promised Land. It cost Saul his kingdom, Samson his sight, Achan his family.

Jerry Bridges explains in *The Pursuit of Holiness*, "Because God is holy, He hates sin. Hate is such a strong word we dislike using it . . . Yet when it comes to God's attitude toward sin, only a strong word such as hate conveys an adequate depth of meaning."[2]

God hates sin. He also knows its destructive effect in our earthly relationships. Jerry McCune became a Christian during his senior year of high school. It was mainly through the influence of his friend Jim, who had become a Christian a few years earlier. Jerry gave up smoking pot soon after accepting Christ. His friends noticed the difference in his lifestyle.

Three months later all the seniors went to the Texas gulf coast for a weekend graduation party. There was plenty to see, to eat, to drink, to smoke. Jerry convinced Jim to get high, and the two of them spent the weekend stoned. Then came the trip home.

"Getting high had been such a lifestyle for me before I was a Christian," Jerry said. "Suddenly I realized that there was now this tremendous guilt, and I knew I had damaged my witness for Christ before all my classmates. Because of my guilt I went to the Lord and told Him I was wrong."

Jerry's sin wasn't the most heinous known to man. I picked his story not because it is rare, but because it's common. We've all been there. We've been hurt by sin. Our closeness to Christ seems clouded. Our witness to friends is suddenly suspect. They might believe a story about Jesus printed in the *New York Times*, but in the *National Enquirer*? Credibility crashes.

Sin. It feels good, and we do it. Like Adam and Eve, we think we can know evil and yet not be overcome by it. But we do not become like God. God knows of the existence of evil, yet God is not evil nor does He give in to evil. We, on the other hand, are attracted to it, and we give in to it.

Don't Lick the Knife!

Eskimo tribesmen bothered by wolves found an effective deterrent against the predators. They would select a long knife and fashion it into a double edge on a grindstone. The edges were then slowly honed to razor sharpness. Next, using a freshly slaughtered animal, they would dip the blades into blood. The blood quickly froze in the Arctic air, and the process was repeated. Eventually the blade was thickly covered, and only smelled of one thing—

blood. The knife was taken out to a spot frequented by wolves and forced blade-up into the ice.

A prowling wolf would eventually notice the faint smell. His eyes would confirm what his nose suspected: There was blood to be had. It was very appealing. His coarse tongue would scour through the layers of frozen nourishment. The wolf would find his appetite whetted as he also tasted a small trickle of fresh blood. He would attack the knife with fervor as the volume of blood, his own blood, increased and dripped from his mouth. His feeding would grow frenzied. The next day the Eskimo could return to his knife and find the frozen carcass of a wolf.

Gruesome. But it's a picture of the effect of sin in our lives. Aren't there equally gruesome consequences? Deteriorated health, shattered marriages, battered children. Or seemingly insignificant consequences: We don't sleep as well or laugh as often or share as openly. Sin costs. Fleeting acquaintance turns into frenzied attachment. It becomes a fatal attraction.

Once we understand the awfulness of sin, we will be less tolerant of it in our own lives. When Paul led people in the city of Ephesus to believe in Christ, a remarkable event occurred. As a result of their faith they renounced some old practices: "Many of the believers who had been practicing black magic confessed their deeds and brought their incantation books and charms and burned them at a public bonfire. (Someone estimated the value of the books at $10,000.)" (Acts 19:18,19)

Those new Christians recognized that their old habits were incompatible with their new lives. I have watched new Christians smash old record albums and throw out magazines and posters. Some have given up a relationship or left a job that forced them to compromise. For others it means turning down invitations to get high with friends, or planning an alternative to an evening at

the bars with the guys. It is all part of your lifelong journey with Christ. Following Him demands that we deal with
our old habits and struggles.

The Guilty Party

Whenever you sin, God's Spirit inside you is
grieved. Sometimes He'll cause you to feel guilty. In sin-
ning, you are choosing at that instant to live independently
of the Lord's will for you. That doesn't cause God to hate
you. He still loves you. But it saddens Him: "And do not
grieve the Holy Spirit of God, with whom you were sealed
for the day of redemption," Paul wrote (Ephesians 4:30,
NIV). To understand how sin does affect you, let's look at
the difference between your *relationship* with God and your
fellowship with God.

Your Relationship With God	Your Fellowship With God
Began when you received Christ (John 1:12).	Began when you received Christ (Colossians 2:6).
Everlasting (1 Peter 1:3,4).	Can be hindered (Psalm 32:3-5).
Maintained solely by God (John 10:27-29).	Maintained in part by you (1 John 1:9).
Never changes (Hebrews 13:5).	Changes when you sin (Psalm 66:18).

Sin does not affect God's eternal relationship with
you—that was established when you trusted in Christ's
payment for your sins. Christ died for all your sins—past,
present and future—nearly 2,000 years ago. At that time,
your entire life was in the future. So, He paid for all the
sins you will ever commit. You are totally forgiven, totally
pardoned.

But if sin doesn't alter God's eternal relationship

with you, how does it affect your fellowship with God? (Fellowship means your earthly, moment-by-moment association.) Sin affects your communication with Him, your witness and your usefulness in doing His will.

Remember the verse quoted earlier about God being light? That's found in 1 John 1:5. The next verse says: "If we claim to have fellowship with him yet walk in the darkness, we lie and do not live by the truth" (1 John 1:6, NIV). Or, as *The Living Bible* paraphrases: "So if we say we are his friends, but go on living in spiritual darkness and sin, we are lying." Sin dulls you to the things Christ wants you to be thinking about and to be doing.

You may notice from the chart that your fellowship with God is hindered when you sin. Psalm 32:3-5 says:

> There was a time when I wouldn't admit what a sinner I was. But my dishonesty made me miserable and filled my days with frustration. All day and all night your hand was heavy on me. My strength evaporated like water on a sunny day until I finally admitted all my sins to you and stopped trying to hide them. I said to myself, "I will confess them to the Lord." And you forgave me! All my guilt is gone.

The psalmist had the correct response to sin. He didn't deny sin. He didn't become preoccupied with it. He confessed it.

Confessing Sin and Repenting

What does it mean to confess sins and repent? First, confession means to agree with God. He already knows you've sinned, so you might as well be honest! First John 1:9 says, "If we confess our sins, he is faithful and just and will forgive us our sins and purify us from all unrighteousness" (NIV).

Being honest about sin doesn't mean a begrudging

admission of "Yeah, I sinned. So what?" Confession means freely admitting our sin and accepting God's attitude about our sin.

Contrary to popular opinion, confession does not mean abjectly begging God for forgiveness. Christ already paid the penalty for all of our sins, and God's forgiveness is available automatically when we confess our sin. The reason God can make this forgiveness available to you instantly is Christ's death on the cross, not the strength or humility with which you confess your sin.

Repentance means to change your actions concerning your sin. It involves agreeing with God that you were wrong and that you do not want to continue to commit that sin.

When I drive in a different city, I invariably find one-way streets by trial and error. Especially error. So I "repent." That means I stop, acknowledge my error and head in the opposite direction.

Repentance may involve restitution as well. If I have stolen from someone, I will need to ask his forgiveness and repay what I have stolen.

But I Still Feel Guilty!

There will be times when you still feel guilty even after you've confessed your sin. It somehow *seems* spiritual to berate ourselves for committing such an awful sin, and we think that if we can lower ourselves in our own eyes, God will be pleased with our humility.

In reality, that attitude displeases God. Part of confession is thanksgiving: thanking God that all of our sins have been paid for by Christ on the cross 2,000 years ago. Thanksgiving involves faith because you are responding to what God's Word says is true about you instead of how you feel. To berate yourself focuses on your sin rather than on Christ and His forgiveness.

Another pitfall comes from mistaking temptation for sin. Everyone is tempted. Even Christ was tempted, but He did not give in to His temptations. He did not sin. If you are being tempted by lust or worry or anger, don't chastise yourself for being a bad Christian. Those tempting thoughts will probably be with you for the rest of your life. But you can choose not to dwell on them and not to give in to them. You can't prevent birds from flying over your head, but you can prevent them from nesting in your hair. Don't feel guilty about being tempted.

Sometimes, though, our guilt is real. God may use guilt constructively in our lives to remind us that we have sinned, but He doesn't mean to destroy us with guilt. Too often we destroy ourselves.

Psychiatrist O. Quentin Hyder, noting that more than half of his Christian patients have guilt in their symptom complex, writes: "Some failure, dishonesty, laziness, thoughtlessness, lack of love, or selfish act—chronically infecting the mind and emotions from years back—leads to guilt feelings which cripple and even destroy a person's peace within."[3]

God has completely forgiven you of all the things you have done. He doesn't look back now on your sins or your failures with condemnation, and neither should you. The cloud of guilt is gone! Accept God's complete forgiveness. Author Larry Richards explains:

> Have you been disappointed in yourself and ashamed of your failure to follow Jesus as fully as you wish? You are forgiven.
>
> Have you made choices that you knew were wrong and come to feel that you've lost all right to hope for God's mercy? You're forgiven.
>
> Have you pushed yourself to do the "right thing" because you felt you ought to, or to avoid the anguish of guilt? You're forgiven.

Have you built walls of self-righteousness to protect you from the failures you're too ashamed to face and to admit? You're forgiven.

Have you been bitter and critical of others, disappointed in them and angry at them at the same time? You're forgiven . . . and so are they.

So live as a forgiven person.[4]

There is someone, however, who would love to see us grovel in misery about our sin. In the courtroom of heaven there is the prosecuting attorney: Satan. His name means "the accuser." He quickly points out our sin to God and says, "Look at this guy! Do you see what he did today? And he claims to be a Christian! You can't possibly forgive him, can You?" Satan peers across the room, and his cold look reminds us that we are guilty.

But we shouldn't feel defeated. In the courtroom with us is Jesus Christ, our advocate. He stands to His feet and says calmly, "Yes, my client did commit sin. But I have already paid for it in full."

Jesus Christ is our representative. John tells us that Jesus is there to plead on our behalf because "He is the one who took God's wrath against our sins upon himself . . ." (1 John 2:2).

God does not want you to live in constant fear and guilt. The Christian life is a life of freedom: freedom from guilt and freedom to live as God intends, which is ultimately the most satisfying life. It is a process of growth, of becoming like Christ and reflecting Christ. And it takes time to grow!

The best way to help the growth process is to read what Abraham Lincoln called "the best gift God has ever given to man." In the next chapter we'll learn more about this gift — the Bible.

Growing Deeper...

Use the following questions to guide your reading of John chapters 11, 12 and 13.

1. Chapter 11: What is Jesus teaching through this miracle? What emotions does Jesus display?

2. Chapter 12: What effect does Lazarus' resurrection have? Who believes in Jesus and why?

3. Chapter 13: How does the principle of serving apply to you?

How to Deal With Sin

1. Ask God to reveal any sin in your life that is unconfessed.

> Search me, O God, and know my heart; test me and know my anxious thoughts. See if there is any offensive way in me, and lead me in the way everlasting (Psalm 139:23,24, NIV).

2. Recognize sin as being against God and His will for you.

> But those who keep on sinning are against God, for every sin is done against the will of God (1 John 3:4).

3. Thank God that He has forgiven you all of your sins.

> If we confess our sins, he is faithful and just and will forgive us our sins and purify us from all unrighteousness (1 John 1:9, NIV).

4. Decide to think and act differently about that sin, dwelling not on how to avoid it, but on Christ and what He wants you to do.

> Do not let any part of your bodies become tools of wickedness, to be used for sinning; but give yourselves completely to God — every part of you — for you are back from death and you want to be tools in the hands of God, to be used for his good purposes (Romans 6:13, NIV).

Recommended Reading

How to Experience God's Love and Forgiveness by Bill Bright (Here's Life Publishers). Studies the great problem of sin and God's great solution of forgiveness.

Chapter 6

Welcome to the Bible!

The Bible is not just for learning;
it's for living.
— Lawrence O. Richards

Would you like to know what God really thinks about you? Or how you should think about God? Welcome to the Bible!

The majesty and infinitude of the Almighty fill its pages. From the dawn of time to the consummation of history, the Bible presents its unerring truth. Years of patient study won't exhaust its contents. Fortunately, you don't have to wait years in order to benefit from Bible reading. You may have already discovered one of the world's best-kept secrets: The Bible can be understood and enjoyed!

Instead of being a dreary old book, the Bible is a captivating drama with authentic heroes and villains. You'll find that it faithfully records the successes and failures of saints and sinners alike. It contains wise sayings and amazing predictions. It speaks of success and celebrating, of suffering and grieving. Principles that apply to marriage, finances, parenting, working—all aspects of life—can be gleaned from its pages.

The Bible is the very personal message of the One who created the universe. Because it is God's living Word, it does more than grab your attention. It speaks to you. In a manner that's almost uncanny, the verses you read today may apply directly to your problems.

For the Word that God speaks is alive and active; it cuts more keenly than any two-edged sword: it strikes through to the place where soul and spirit meet, to the innermost intimacies of a man's being: it examines the very thoughts and motives of a man's heart (Hebrews 4:12, Phillips).

Shortly after I accepted Christ I bought a paperback copy of *The New Testament in Modern English*. I found that its words spoke directly to me. Words about not worrying, forgiveness and love jumped from the pages and spread into my world.

The Bible explains how it was written: "For no prophecy recorded in Scripture was ever thought up by the prophet himself. It was the Holy Spirit within these godly men who gave them true messages from God" (2 Peter 1:20,21). Those verses apply specifically to the Old Testament prophecies, but the entire Bible is inspired: "*All* Scripture is God-breathed . . ." (2 Timothy 3:16, NIV).

The word *inspiration* literally means "God-breathed." From God's very life, His breath, came the words of the Bible. You may find other books inspiring to read because they are intellectually or emotionally moving, but they are not the very words of God. Only the Bible is.

The Bible Reveals

The Bible reveals what God wants you to know about Him and about life. It contains promises: things that God says He will do for you. Here are just a few of God's promises to you:

- God will use everything in your life for good, conforming you into the image of Christ (Romans 8:28,29);
- He will always be with you (Matthew 28:20);
- He will generously give wisdom if you ask (James 1:5);
- He will supply every need in your life (Philippians 4:19);
- He already knows your needs before you ask Him (Matthew 6:32);
- His peace will superintend your thought life as you pray with thankfulness (Philippians 4:4-7).

The Bible also reveals your roots. Alex Haley, author of *Roots*, recalls the summer evenings during his childhood when he sat on the front porch with relatives. His grandma would be sitting in her white rocker, and Alex would plop down beside her. When Grandma started reminiscing, Alex could sense a wall of tension between her and his own mother, particularly if the talk turned to slavery. His mother would interrupt, "Oh, Maw, I *wish* you'd stop all that old-timey slavery stuff, it's entirely embarrassing." His grandmother would snap a reply, "If *you* don't care who and where you come from, well, I does!"[1]

When you spend time in the Bible, you discover who you were before you became a Christian. You learn why habit patterns from the old life must be broken, and why those same temptations may still occur. You also discover who you are now: a new person in Christ. Galatians 2:20 says, "I have been crucified with Christ and I no longer live, but Christ lives in me. The life I live in the body, I live by faith in the Son of God, who loved me and gave himself for me" (NIV).

Augustine, the fourth-century skeptic-turned-Christian thinker, lived as a playboy for a brief period of his life before his conversion. After becoming a Christian, he was once walking down a street and was greeted by a former mistress. Augustine ignored her greeting and continued walking. "Augustine, Augustine, it is I!" she called. "Yes," replied Augustine. "But it is no longer I." Augustine understood he had a new identity in Christ.

The Bible reveals the future. Now it doesn't say who will win next year's World Series or what will happen to the Soviet Union, the United States or Israel in 2095. But the book of Revelation does tell how human history will be consummated in the final triumph of Christ over Satan and evil. It's like those old western movies: You don't know all that's going to happen during the movie, but you know that the good guy will win at the end. As Martin Luther said, "I don't know what the future holds, but I know who holds the future."

Getting Started in the Bible

Have you wondered why we started with the Gospel of John in the "Going Deeper" sections rather than in Genesis? With most books, you learn best by beginning at page 1. You would think that the best place to start your study of the Bible would be on page 1 of Genesis. After all, *Genesis* means "beginnings." But Genesis assumes its readers are conversant with ancient Semitic culture. You may suddenly feel overwhelmed, and the "book of beginnings" could become the end of your Bible reading!

The key to understanding the Bible is Christ. The Old Testament (*testament* means "covenant") looks forward to His coming. The Gospels reveal Christ's identity and mission, and the rest of the New Testament explains the implications of that new life in Christ. To understand the Old Testament, you have to begin in the New Testament.

The Bible is not arranged in strict chronological

order. The books of the Bible are placed in categories. The Old Testament covers the period from the creation of the world (Genesis 1) until the fourth century B.C. The Old Testament books are arranged: Genesis to Esther (historical); Job to Song of Songs (poetic); Isaiah to Malachi (prophetic).

The New Testament covers the comparatively brief period from the birth of Christ until the end of the first century. The New Testament books are arranged: Matthew to Acts (historical); Romans to Jude (didactic); Revelation (apocalyptic).

Pen, Paper and the Holy Spirit

Bible reading is an intellectual exercise, involving your mind. But to understand the spiritual teaching and apply it, you need the Holy Spirit's leading. As you read the Bible, pray, asking God the Holy Spirit to make plain to you what He wants you to know: "But when he, the Spirit of truth, comes, he will guide you into all truth" (John 16:13, NIV).

Develop a spirit of expectancy — God wants to teach you through His Word. But don't rely on feelings. I've had some of the best times of Bible study when I decided that I would continue reading for fifteen more minutes even though the previous fifteen minutes were "boring."

Keep a journal to record what God teaches you. Writing helps organize your thoughts, as well as giving your something you can return to several months later.

A Commitment to a Regular Time

If your Bible study is regular and daily, it will become a habit in your life. Find a place free from distraction. It's tough if your life revolves around a noisy house or a noisy office. Be creative, and pick the time of day when you are most alert and able to spend time with God. Remember, you are pursuing a relationship with God and you want to be able to converse with Him.

Decide to spend fifteen minutes every day this week in the Bible. The time will pass quickly, but it is also short enough that you can keep it in your schedule every day. You want to work on building consistent Bible reading into your life.

A recommendation: The best aid I have found for becoming consistent in reading the Bible is *The 31-Day Experiment* by Dick Purnell (Here's Life Publishers). It guides you not only in what verses to read, but also in what questions to ask in order to understand and apply the Scripture. If you read the Bible each day for a month (thirty-one days), it's likely to become a habit in your life.

The Reliability of His Word

There's an old adage: "Seven days without the Bible makes one weak." Daily reading of the Bible is essential to your spiritual health. Yet Bible reading is often the first thing squeezed out of busy schedules. And we can be lazy! It's easier to turn on the television and turn off our minds.

But there is another reason why the Bible is left unread: There's doubt that the Bible is really true. Perhaps it is full of errors. Maybe only part of it is true. Ever wondered about that?

The greatest assurance for you as a Christian is the knowledge that your faith is supported by a trustworthy God who has given reliable evidence. God has spoken, and He has spoken clearly and authoritatively through His Word.

The Bible is inerrant; it is without error on every subject it addresses. If it contained errors, it couldn't be God's Word, for God cannot err. *I* err plenty in applying, interpreting and teaching it. God doesn't.

Let's look at three common questions about the Bible. Perhaps you've asked yourself these same questions.

1. Isn't the Bible too old to be very reliable?

The Bible is actually a compilation of sixty-six books, written over 1500 years. The books were composed in three major languages: Hebrew, Aramaic and Greek. They were written by forty authors with a variety of backgrounds. Yet the Bible is unified. By comparison, try to put together writings by forty different authors from the same time period writing on the same subject, and see if they agree. The Bible, despite its diverse authorship, shows a unity of thought. You can trace the themes of God's grace and salvation throughout these sixty-six books — without contradictions.

The Bible is not only unique in its authorship and claims to inspiration, it is also historically reliable. Luke, the writer of a Gospel and the book of Acts, has been called "a consummate historian . . . ranked in his own right with the great writers of the Greeks."[2]

The greatest confirmation of the Bible's reliability has come from archaeologists in the twentieth century. William F. Albright, one of this century's greatest archaeologists, has stated: "Discovery after discovery has established the accuracy of innumerable details, and has brought increased recognition to the value of the Bible as a source of history."[3]

2. Hasn't the Bible been changed through translation and retranslation?

A popular misconception about the Bible is that it is a product of repeated translation, with each translation based upon the previous one. Thus the Bible's true message, just like in the children's game of telephone, becomes terribly garbled as errors in translation are compounded through the centuries.

In actuality, our modern translations of the Bible are based upon the results of the science of textual criticism. Scholars study the ancient Greek, Hebrew and Aramaic copies of the Bible. Some of these New Testament copies date from the second century A.D. And many Old Testament manuscripts are far older. From these, scholars arrive at an English translation that is an accurate equivalent of those ancient manuscripts. Instead of being the product of repeated retranslations, they are actually as close to a direct translation from the original manuscripts as possible.

3. Should I interpret the Bible literally?

Paul Little talks about the "literal translation" issue in *Know Why You Believe*:

> Those who accept the Bible as the Word of God are often accused of taking the Bible "literally." As it is usually put, the question, "Do you believe the Bible literally?" is like the question, "Have you stopped beating your wife?" Either a yes or a no convicts the one who responds. Whenever the question is asked, the term "literally" must be carefully defined.[4]

Interpretation involves accepting the plainest meaning of the text within its literary genre. The Psalms are poetry, so their language is often figurative. How else would you understand Psalm 98:8: "Let the rivers clap their hands, let the mountains sing together for joy . . ."? The book of Revelation is apocalyptic; the writer can only use similes in describing the visions: "The first living creature was like a lion, the second was like an ox . . ." Poetic or prophetic genre is often written figuratively and should not be interpreted literally.

Yet much of the Bible's literature is historical narrative. Its language is literal, not figurative. When John tells us that Jesus rose from the dead, he does not mean that the memory of Jesus' faith was resurrected in the consciousness of the disciples. Jesus' resurrection was physical. After He was raised from the dead He spoke with His followers, walked with them, ate with them. That may seem unbelievable to skeptics today (it was unbelievable to many then), but John meant what he wrote to be taken literally.

Start Today

The best way to start getting into God's Word is to just do it. There will be times when everything you read seems to be written just for you. But there will be times when nothing makes sense and reading becomes dry. The key is to keep reading.

You can make a thousand excuses not to read the Bible, but if you really want to know God in a personal way, there's no other alternative. God will honor the time you spend with Him, and you'll find yourself growing in your faith. It will be time well spent.

There is another important element vital to our growth in our relationship with God. It's a privilege that we, as children of God, have alone. As we will see in the next chapter, we can talk honestly and confidently with the God of the universe.

Growing Deeper...

Read the Gospel of John, chapters 8, 9 and 10.

1. In chapters 8 and 9: Underline *sin*. How does Jesus use this word? How do the religious leaders use it?

2. In chapter 10: What does Jesus teach about life?

How to Choose a Bible Translation

With nearly a dozen versions of the Bible to choose from, which one is best for you? Both the *New International Version* and *The Living Bible* are used in this book.

Where no translation is listed, the verses you read are quoted from *The Living Bible*. Where you see the letters "NIV," the verse is quoted from the *New International Version*.

The *New International Version* is a very readable and accurate translation of the original texts. *The Living Bible* is extremely readable but strives for a thought-for-thought paraphrase rather than a word-for-word translation of the original manuscripts.

Consider purchasing a study Bible such as the *NIV Study Bible*, the *Ryrie Study Bible*, or the *Open Bible*. These are not appreciably more expensive than a non-study edition, and they are available in several translations.

Study Bibles give you a wealth of information on a particular book as well as providing footnotes that help you interpret verses that are hard to understand. You may want to purchase a hardcover edition: It's cheaper than a leather edition, and it may encourage you to write notes in it often.

Recommended Reading

A Guide to Understanding Your Bible by Josh Mc-Dowell (Here's Life Publishers). Build a lifetime of Bible study using a simple, five-step approach. Includes sample studies.

The Christian and the Bible by Bill Bright (Here's Life Publishers). Discover why the Bible is reliable and how to incorporate daily study into your life.

Knowing Scripture by R. C. Sproul (InterVarsity Press). Sproul explains why and how to study the Bible, and gives principles to help you interpret the passages you study.

Creative Bible Study by Lawrence O. Richards (Zondervan Publishers). Richards helps you discover the Bible as God's living word, explaining your new identity in

Christ and the joy of Bible study.

The 31-Day Experiment Series by Dick Purnell (Here's Life Publishers). These Bible study booklets guide you through a month's worth of selected Scriptures on topics such as faith, the names of God, witnessing, and how to stand for God before the world.

Chapter 7

Communicating With God

Does prayer really work?

My wife Sarah and I were reassigned several years ago by Campus Crusade for Christ to direct the student ministry at University of North Texas. We had sold our home in Indiana earlier that spring and would be giving the buyer possession of it in six weeks. I needed to locate and buy a house during a three-day visit to the university, and Sarah, as joint buyer, would be approving my purchase sight unseen.

Sarah gave me a list of items she was praying for in a house: three bedrooms, two-car garage, separate laundry room, beige or brown carpeting to match our furniture, a patio and fenced-in backyard for the kids, and a gas grill. Plus she desired Christian neighbors with children the same age as our own. I laughed when I saw her list but told her I'd be praying too.

We now have a three-bedroom home with a two-car garage, brown and beige carpeting, patio, a fenced-in backyard—and a gas grill. (We didn't get the separate laundry room.) Our neighbor is a pastor who has one child about the same age as our oldest daughter. It was by far the most affordable of any house I viewed and was available for oc-cupancy the same week we needed to move to Texas.

Is "answered prayer" just a fancy name for what some might call coincidence? Dan Hayes, National Col-legiate Prayer Alliance director, says, "When I receive answers to prayer, some people say 'Well, that's just a coin-cidence.' All I know is that when I pray, coincidences happen, and when I don't pray, they don't happen. So I'll just keep praying for coincidences."

Everyone has probably prayed at some point in their life. The prayer may have been an appeal for help to Whoever Is Up There. Perhaps it was a prayer in a church service. But simply to have prayed is not to experience prayer as God intends. Prayer is a vital part of your new relationship with Jesus Christ.

I'm certainly not an expert on prayer — I'm still learning! But over the years I have become convinced that God, because of prayer, changes things. Let's look at some characteristics of prayer that may help us to understand that fact.

Prayer Is Honest Communication

After teaching His disciples "the Lord's prayer," Jesus taught them this principle:

> So I say to you: Ask and it will be given to you; seek and you will find; knock and the door will be opened to you. For everyone who asks receives; he who seeks finds; and to him who knocks, the door will be opened. Which of you fathers, if your son asks for a fish, will give him a snake instead? Or if he asks for an egg, will give him a scorpion? If you then, though you are evil, know how to give good gifts to your children, how much more will your Father in heaven give the Holy Spirit to those who ask him! (Luke 11:9-13, NIV)

Honesty in your communication with God brings freedom. You may feel like presenting a false front to the rest of the world, but you don't need to hide anything from God. Some of my best times in prayer occur when I tell God, "I don't really feel like praying today, but I am going to pray because You are my God and I am going to spend time with You." After I have cleared the air, I can then talk to God and learn from Him.

Did you ever feel afraid to pray? Afraid that God would either not answer your prayer or would twist your request into a "scorpion"? God loves you! He sent Christ to die for your sins because He loves you. He won't reject you if you pray something off the wall. He wants to spend time with you!

Prayer isn't just for "spiritual" matters. Whether it is a family situation, a business deal or a need that would seem trifling to everyone else, God desires that you talk to Him about it. The apostle Paul says, "Don't worry about anything; instead, pray about everything; tell God your needs and don't forget to thank him for his answers" (Philippians 4:6).

Think of exactly what you need as you pray, and then mention it to God. If you are looking for another job in the field of accounting, tell God exactly what you are looking for, just as you would a close friend. Don't pray generally, "Lord, I need a job," when you know you aren't hoping for a career running the cash register at McDonald's. (Although every job is a wonderful opportunity to serve God!)

It's better to pray honestly and specifically than to secretly desire something and not talk to the Lord about it. After you talk to God about what you want, you can begin to let Him give you what you ask — or let Him change your desires. Give God the freedom to change your response to circumstances even if He doesn't change the circumstances. Praying "Your will be done" means you want His will accomplished more than your own.

Prayer Is Reverent

Honesty with God doesn't imply flippancy with God. We still revere Him. To revere, according to Webster's, means "to show devoted deferential honor to."

God is infinitely different from finite man. God is not the product of a man's need for a god. God is not a projection of man by an exponential factor of 1,000. "God," as one theologian has remarked, "is not man shouting in a loud voice." The prophet Isaiah recorded these words from God: "I am the LORD, and there is no other; apart from me there is no God" (Isaiah 45:5a, NIV).

But why emphasize this? First, without a proper view of God's character, we pray weakly. It's as if we have God all figured out and keep Him in a neat little box for our use. But should a great crisis in our life occur, our God-in-a-box is not big enough to handle it. He lacks the justice to correct wrongs and the power to enable us to live through the toughest times.

Second, prayer is a means of talking, not taking. O. Hallesby, a Norwegian theologian, says we all grow up thinking "How can I, in the best way, make use of God for my own personal advantage? How can I make Him serve me best now, in the future and throughout all eternity?"[1] This "God's on my side" attitude is totally inconsistent with Christian prayer. Seek the Giver, not the gifts.

Prayer Is Thankful

So do not worry, saying, "What shall we eat?" or "What shall we drink?" or "What shall we wear?" For the pagans run after all these things, and your heavenly Father knows that you need them. But seek first his kingdom and his righteousness, and all these things will be given to you as well (Matthew 6:31-33, NIV).

If I understand that God provides for my needs, I will be thankful in prayer and won't have to worry. Paul, in writing to a church that had given sacrificially to sponsor his ministry, was convinced that God in turn would supply the needs of that church: "And my God will meet all your needs according to his glorious riches in Christ Jesus" (Philippians 4:19, NIV). As you read the Bible, try underlining the verses that mention God's provisions for your needs. You may find yourself giving thanks to God.

Prayer Is Confident

The book of Hebrews says, "Let us then approach the throne of grace with confidence, so that we may receive mercy and find grace to help us in our time of need" (Hebrews 4:16, NIV).

Like an earthly parent, God enjoys communication with His children. As His children, we can approach Him with confidence: "And so we should not be like cringing, fearful slaves, but we should behave like God's very own children, adopted into the bosom of his family, and calling to him 'Father, Father' " (Romans 8:15).

The all-knowing God loves you as His child. Christ, who could say to the Father, "All I have is yours, and all you have is mine," says to you: "If you remain in me and my words remain in you, ask whatever you wish, and it will be given you" (John 17:10; 15:7, NIV).

Honesty, thankfulness and confidence are marks of prayer that the world finds unusual, to say the least. Do you honestly believe God listens to *you*? It would be hard to believe so, but the Bible makes it very clear:

And we are sure of this, that he will listen to us whenever we ask him for anything in line with his will. And if we really know he is listening when we talk to him and make our requests, then we can be sure that he will answer us (1 John 5:14,15).

Prayer that A.C.T.S.

Prayer is intimate communication with the majestic God. That's very exciting! Sometimes, though, our communication gets bogged down. We tend to become repetitious or half-hearted, wondering if our prayers are going past the ceiling. It happens to everyone.

I've discovered one way to keep my prayers vital and meaningful. I use the acronym A.C.T.S. It stands for:

Adoration

Confession

Thanksgiving

Supplication

Adoration means revering God. Tell God you appreciate Him more for who He is than for what He does for you. You may discover, as I have, that many of your prayers have been centered around yourself and your needs. To break this habit, spend time thanking God for His character. Read some of the Psalms of adoration aloud—to God (e.g., Psalm 100; 103-105; 145-50).

Confession of sin isn't limited to the times you set aside for prayer, but there ought to be the assurance that there is no unconfessed sin when you do pray. Take time to be quiet and ask God to point out anything displeasing to Him. Confess whatever He points out.

Thanksgiving. I'm not a very thankful person by nature. But I find it easy to thank God when I begin to look back and remember what He has done. It's great for regaining perspective during those times I feel in the pits.

Supplication involves bringing requests to God,

both on your behalf and others. Supplication is usually what we think of when someone mentions prayer.

When prayer includes adoration, confession, thanksgiving and supplication, a curious thing takes place. Our own needs appear in a different light. The majestic God has taken care of us before; He can be trusted now. This becomes even more apparent if we keep a written record of requests and answers.

I write down some of my prayer requests in a notebook as a permanent record of what God has done. Exactly *how* you keep a written record of your requests and God's answers is up to you. The simple method I use is:

Date	My Request	Related Scripture	Answer

By "related Scripture" I mean those verses that may apply to a particular prayer request. Be careful, though. Like so many things, it's easier to say, "I want it—I'll get it!" rather than "I want it—does God want it for me?"

Supplication also involves praying for others. It's very likely that someone you know was praying for you in the months and weeks before you accepted Christ. You can be involved in the process of helping your friends know Christ by talking to them about God and talking to God about them.

How would you like to travel around the world and help people? You can through prayer. You can be in the boardroom of America's corporations, with the hungry in sub-Sahara Africa, in the offices of top Soviet leaders—all through prayer. You can pray for businessmen to make ethical decisions; for bountiful crops in Ethiopia; for Soviet leaders to know Jesus Christ and give political freedom to the people. Try making a brief list from the evening news or morning paper of people and situations to pray for.

He Bends Down and Listens

If you spend time with Christians who have a strong prayer life, you will notice that they have an attitude of expectancy. They actually expect God to hear and answer their prayers! They can identify with the writer of Psalm 116, who said, "I love the Lord because he hears my prayers and answers them. Because he bends down and listens, I will pray as long as I breathe!" (Psalm 116:1,2)

It's not that expectant people are natural-born optimists; they have simply chosen to believe what God says about prayer: "And I will do whatever you ask in my name, so that the Son may bring glory to the Father. You may ask me for anything in my name, and I will do it" (John 14:13,14, NIV).

Expectant people aren't surprised when God answers prayers. They believe in His promises and rely on His strength. And we'll be talking more about a spirit of dependency on the Lord in the next chapter!

Growing Deeper...

1. Read John 17. Try to title each of the following passages: Verses 1-5; Verses 6-19; Verses 20-26. What type of relationship with His Father is reflected in these verses? How confident does Jesus seem that His prayer will be answered?

2. Reading about prayer will not substitute for prayer. Do you have a notebook available to record prayer requests? Record the following: two needs in your life today; two needs in the life of a friend or family member. Date the requests and pray about them each day this week.

Recommended Reading

Quiet Talks on Prayer by S. D. Gordon (Baker Press). Gordon explains the purpose of prayer, why we often fail in prayer, and how to pray.

The Kneeling Christian. Anonymous (Zondervan Press). A short, insightful classic that explains how to pray powerfully.

The Christian and Prayer by Bill Bright (Here's Life Publishers). A practical and easy-to-follow Bible study booklet emphasizing the purpose and privilege of prayer.

How To Pray by Bill Bright (Here's Life Publishers). Bright answers several vital questions about prayer: Who can pray? Why are we to pray? To whom do we pray? When should we pray? What should be included in prayer? How can we pray with confidence?

Chapter 8

The Christian's Secret

Discovering the key to consistency
in your spiritual life.

Have you ever wondered why so many Christians don't act like Christians?

I had met my friend Mike for lunch and was listening to his doubts about Christianity. Mike didn't doubt his new Christian faith; he just doubted Christians.

"I haven't met very many people who seem to really live the Christian life," Mike said. "My Christian co-workers sure don't act differently than the non-Christians at the office. My wife and I have visited a few churches, and people seem to be there just for show. It all kind of bums me out."

Mike had surveyed the pristine faces of co-workers across church sanctuaries. He had also observed their demeanor during late nights as their engineering department pushed to meet project deadlines. Sunday morning veneers can't withstand the jolts and bruises of life. They tend to peel off under pressure and reveal inconsistencies.

Several months after becoming a Christian, I found

a Bible passage that depicted all of my struggles with consistency. It pierced the veneer of religion in my own life and exposed the problem:

> I don't understand myself at all, for I really want to do what is right, but I can't. I do what I don't want to — what I hate. I know perfectly well that what I am doing is wrong, and my bad conscience proves that I agree with these laws I am breaking. But I can't help myself, because I'm no longer doing it. It is sin inside me that is stronger than I am that makes me do these evil things.
>
> I know I am rotten through and through so far as my old sinful nature is concerned. No matter which way I turn I can't make myself do right. I want to but I can't. When I want to do good, I don't; and when I try not to do wrong, I do it anyway. Now if I am doing what I don't want to, it is plain where the trouble is: sin still has me in its evil grasp.
>
> It seems to be a fact of life that when I want to do what is right, I inevitably do what is wrong. I love to do God's will so far as my new nature is concerned; but there is something else deep within me, in my lower nature, that is at war with my mind and wins the fight and makes me a slave to the sin that is still within me. In my mind I want to be God's willing servant but instead I find myself still enslaved to sin.
>
> So you see how it is: my new life tells me to do right, but the old nature that is still inside me loves to sin. Oh, what a terrible predicament I'm in! Who will free me from my slavery to this deadly lower nature? Thank God! It has been done by Jesus Christ our Lord. He has set me free (Romans 7:15-25).

I certainly could identify with the problem Paul wrote about in these verses, but what was the solution he had found? How had Paul been set free from slavery to his "lower nature"? I certainly didn't feel set free. I felt a lot more like Sisyphus, that pathetic figure in Greek mythology. After he betrayed a secret of Zeus, Sisyphus was condemned to spend his life forcing a huge boulder up to the top of a mountain, only to have it tumble over him and roll back each time to the bottom. Ever feel like that?

At first the Christian life seems difficult; soon it seems impossible. Who can honestly say that he loves his enemies, that he forgives those who hurt him? Do we really want to be delivered from temptations—or just the consequences of sin? Do we submit to authority? Do we worry or lust?

Does anyone really expect you to live the Christian life? God does! And He has made the seemingly impossible, possible: "For I can do everything God asks me to with the help of Christ who gives me the strength and power" (Philippians 4:13).

The Christian's secret to a consistent life is for Christ to live His life through us: "I have been crucified with Christ: and I myself no longer live, but Christ lives in me. And the real life I now have within this body is a result of my trusting in the Son of God, who loved me and gave himself for me" (Galatians 2:20).

It was during Christ's final evening with His disciples that He told them He would be leaving them, but they would not be left alone: "But the fact of the matter is that it is best for you that I go away, for if I don't, the Comforter won't come. If I do, he will—for I will send him to you" (John 16:7).

The usage of *Comforter* dates back to John Wycliffe, a fourteenth-century translator of the Bible. In Wycliffe's day, *comforter* meant someone who helped another to be brave. You have been given someone to enable you to live the Christian life bravely—the Holy Spirit. He isn't just a guide at the information booth along the heavenly trail: He is the Spirit of Christ—come to live in you.

Who Is the Holy Spirit?

The Holy Spirit is God, as are the Son and the Father. Much of the confusion surrounding the Holy Spirit occurs when people fail to view Him as a person. He has a personality. He is not the personification of intense religious feelings, nor is He a ghost. He is a divine person with a will and emotions.

The Holy Spirit possesses all the attributes that the Son and the Father have. He is omnipotent (all powerful), omniscient (all knowing), immutable (unchanging) and eternal. He is the third person of the trinity.

The word *trinity* is not found in the Bible but is often used to describe the relationship between the three persons of the Godhead—Father, Son and Holy Spirit. They are not three separate Gods because God is one (Deuteronomy 6:4; 1 Timothy 2:5,6). But they are three distinct persons with three different roles in one divine nature.

You may be wondering, *How can three be one?* God in His totality is inscrutable; we can understand only what He reveals to us. Our knowledge of Him is not complete, but it is sufficient. We can't fully understand the Trinity. But to deny the Trinity is to relegate the Son or the Holy Spirit (or both) to a position inferior to God the Father. There's an old saying: "Try to understand the Trinity and you may lose your mind; deny the Trinity and you may lose your soul."

What Is the Purpose of the Holy Spirit?

The Holy Spirit is a major part of your Christian life. Let's examine some of His roles and see why He is so important.

It was the Holy Spirit who convicted you of your sin and your need for Christ (John 16:8-11). The Bible explains that without the Holy Spirit's help, people think Christianity is foolish (1 Corinthians 1:18). Those around you think it's crazy you've made such a commitment to Christ! You don't see it that way at all because the Holy Spirit has revealed the wonder of a life in Christ to you.

The Holy Spirit gave you new life. He regenerated you. Flesh gives birth only to flesh, Jesus said. It takes the Holy Spirit to give a spiritual birth (John 3:6). And it is through that Spirit that God's love was poured into your heart (Romans 5:5). The Holy Spirit also provides an inner witness (an assurance) that you are a Christian (Romans 8:16).

The Holy Spirit is a teacher and enabler. He leads you to the truth of God's Word. He illuminates, or throws light upon, the Bible so you are able to understand and apply its truth (John 16:13,14). He enables you to witness, giving you both power and spiritual effectiveness in your witnessing (Acts 1:8). He intercedes for you before the Father when you feel like you don't know what or how to pray (Romans 8:26,27).

Does the Holy Spirit's role seem a bit clearer now? He was sent by Christ to enable you to live the Christian life! As Paul wrote, ". . . the Spirit of him who raised Jesus from the dead is living in you" (Romans 8:11, NIV). The Christian life is possible only with the power of the Holy Spirit.

Through this empowering, you will be able to obey Christ. No one who disobeys God's Word can claim that God is leading him. To love Christ *always* involves obedience. What we choose to think about, how we spend the time and money God has entrusted to us, how we respond to others' needs — simple obedience shows God we love Him.

All of this brings glory to God, and that is the Holy Spirit's ultimate purpose! John 16:14 says, "He will bring glory to me by taking from what is mine and making it known to you" (NIV). Some Christians refer to the Spirit-controlled life as "the Christ-centered life." The Holy Spirit centers our life on the things that please Christ.

You may be thinking, *I need the Holy Spirit in my life!* If you are a Christian, He is already there: "You are controlled by your new nature if you have the Spirit of God living in you. (And remember that if anyone doesn't have the Spirit of Christ living in him, he is not a Christian at all)" (Romans 8:9). The Holy Spirit resides in you, but you may not be yielding your life to His direction. He may be a resident — without being president.

A look at the problems in the church in Corinth nearly 2,000 years ago may help clarify the role of the Holy Spirit in your life. The people at Corinth were Christians who weren't acting like Christians. There was a divisive spirit. They tolerated sexual immorality among the church members because it was so prevalent in their culture. They were extremely proud of their spiritual knowledge and experiences. It was aberrant Christianity.

So Paul wrote to them to remind them that they were to act in a holy way because their bodies were now home to the Holy Spirit: "Haven't you yet learned that your body is the home of the Holy Spirit God gave you, and that he lives within you?" (1 Corinthians 6:19) He told them God wanted unity, not division, in the church. And spiritual knowledge and experiences mean nothing without mature love. Yet Paul didn't accuse them of lacking the Holy Spirit. The Holy Spirit wasn't absent, but His work was suppressed by sin.

Paul distinguished between two types of Christians: the spiritual Christian and the carnal Christian.

1. The Spiritual Christian

The spiritual man makes judgments about all things, but he himself is not subject to any man's judgment . . . (1 Corinthians 2:15, NIV).

The spiritual person has accepted Christ and lives a Christ-centered life. He is not sinless, though, and he faces problems and temptations every day, just like everyone else. But as a way of life, he trusts Christ with each detail and problem that comes along. His greatest desire is to please Christ, and he doesn't rely on the approval of others.

The spiritual Christian may not be a famous Christian. She is the receptionist who seems to always have time for people. He is the lawyer who devotes Thursday evenings to gluing Bible verses onto cardboard trees for his kids' Sunday school class after ten hours of phone calls and deadlines at the law firm. She is the account executive who uses biblical principles in relating to her clients and employees. He is the Little League coach who models good sportsmanship on and off the field. She is the mother who prays as she cleans, chauffeurs her kids, entertains guests and collapses at night with her worn Bible turned a page past yesterday's reading.

No one set of activities characterizes the spiritual Christian. A Christ-centered life shows itself in many ways through a person's actions and attitudes. A spiritual Christian reflects Christ in his daily life—even in how he responds to disappointments, failures and sins.

2. The Carnal Christian

Brothers, I could not address you as spiritual but as worldly—mere infants in Christ. I gave you milk, not solid food, for you were not yet ready for it. Indeed, you are still not ready. You are still worldly. For since there is jealousy and quarreling among you, are you not worldly? Are you not acting like mere men? (1 Corinthians 3:1-3, NIV)

Carnal means "fleshly." The carnal Christian *is* a Christian (he has committed his life to Jesus Christ at some point), but his life is oriented around himself and his needs.

He may show some evidence of being a Christian, but the work of the Holy Spirit is suppressed either through conscious disobedience or ignorance of the Spirit's ministry.

What distinguishes the carnal Christian from the spiritual Christian? It isn't that the carnal Christian lacks part of Christ or the Holy Spirit—he possesses the same spiritual resources as the spiritual Christian. But the spiritual man relies on Christ's power to live his Christian life while the carnal man relies on his own power.

When things are going well in life, it may be easy to mask your spiritual condition. But under pressure, your true condition emerges. Are you uptight or angry? Do you worry about the future? Trying to live the Christian life on your own efforts is as futile as trying to get around town by pushing your car.

Learning to use the power of the Holy Spirit is like stepping into that car you've been pushing around and finding the key that will turn on the ignition and release the horsepower of the engine. The Bible calls that key the filling of the Holy Spirit.

What Is the Filling of the Holy Spirit?

Knowledge about the Holy Spirit isn't synonymous with the filling of the Holy Spirit. Those Christians whom Paul wrote to in 1 Corinthians knew about the Holy Spirit. They had so much knowledge that they were proud of it. God isn't impressed by the *accumulation* of knowledge; He looks for the *application* of knowledge—actually giving the Holy Spirit control of your life, the "filling of the Spirit."

The Bible talks about being "led" by the Spirit. That implies we obey what He says: He leads, we follow. Simple enough. But usually we don't like anyone telling us what to do—even if it's God! Yet the filling of the Holy Spirit means allowing the Spirit of God through the Word of God to tell us what to do.

We have the choice each day: Will we let the Holy Spirit fill us, or will we be controlled by something else? Will fear about the future, or our desire to get what we want, become more important than obeying Christ? When the Holy Spirit fills you, He controls your thoughts and your actions. You can't be filled with hatred, fear or worry while you are filled with the Spirit. There isn't room.

Paul, in a letter to the Christians at Ephesus, contrasts the filling of the Holy Spirit with being drunk:

> Don't act thoughtlessly, but try to find out and do whatever the Lord wants you to. Don't drink too much wine, for many evils lie along that path; be filled instead with the Holy Spirit, and controlled by him (Ephesians 5:17).

If you are drunk, you have allowed another force to take control of you. You may think or act differently: Suddenly you are friends with everybody; you gain instant courage to tackle any obstacle—even if it's a table and chairs. You still have the same identity, but you have been changed.

Unlike alcohol, the changes the Holy Spirit produces aren't artificial. They don't wear off with time. The Bible calls these lasting changes the fruit that is produced from a Christ-centered life: "But when the Holy Spirit controls our lives he will produce this kind of fruit in us: love, joy, peace, patience, kindness, goodness, faithfulness, gentleness and self-control; and here there is no conflict with Jewish laws" (Galatians 5:22,23).

How Can I be Filled With the Holy Spirit?

The control of the Holy Spirit is our choice. It's voluntary, but it's not by osmosis. People don't become drunk by handling unopened cases of beer or working in a liquor store. It's after drinking the liquor that things suddenly get fuzzy. As a Christian you can be surrounded by Bibles and Christians without being filled with the Holy Spirit. Or you can be alone, but Spirit-filled.

You can express your desire to follow the Holy Spirit's control through prayer. Here is a prayer that has often been helpful to me:

> "Dear Father, I need You. I acknowledge that I have been directing my own life and that, as a result, I have sinned against You. I thank You that You have forgiven my sins through Christ's death on the cross for me. I now invite Christ to again take His place on the throne of my life. Fill me with the Holy Spirit as You commanded me to be filled, and as You promised in Your Word that You would do if I asked in faith. I pray this in the name of Jesus. As an expression of my faith, I now thank You for directing my life and for filling me with the Holy Spirit."[1]

If you prayed that prayer, desiring the Spirit's control, then the Holy Spirit fills you now—even if you don't feel like it. Remember when you committed your life to Christ? You may have had a very emotional experience, or you may have been like me—I felt nothing unusual after accepting Christ. Christ came in not because of a feeling, but because God's Word is true. It's the same with the filling of the Spirit.

Some people equate the filling of the Holy Spirit with a mystical religious experience. It's not mystical. It is a decision of faith: a response to what God says in His Word. Being filled with the Holy Spirit isn't dependent upon the feelings you receive, but upon the Bible you believe.

Three Questions

The ministry of the Holy Spirit is so vital to our Christian life! There may be several questions that remain unanswered in your mind.

1. Why aren't more Christians filled with the Spirit?

That was really Mike's question that day we lunched together. What is the reason more Christians aren't filled with the Holy Spirit?

In a word, *sin*. We choose to disobey God. This can take the form of pride: wanting things our way. We don't give God control of our finances; we've worked hard for our money and it's ours now. We don't give God control of our relationships; why forgive that person when it's really their fault? We don't give God control of our personal morality; that's nobody's business but our own — not even God's. That's pride talking. Scripture says, "He [God] mocks proud mockers but gives grace to the humble" (Proverbs 3:34, NIV).

Sin can take another form: *fear*. Proverbs states, "Fear of man will prove to be a snare . . . " (Proverbs 29:25, NIV). Is there something that God wants you to do, but you haven't done it because you're afraid of what people will think? I know it's easy for me to think, *I can't do that. I would look foolish if I did that. God can't possibly want me to do that.* But often, He does!

The last half of that verse in Proverbs teaches: "but whoever trusts in the LORD is kept safe." It's easy to put the approval of people above the approval of God, but isn't pleasing God what we really want? Our lives will be different than other peoples'. But it's worth it.

2. Can I be filled with the Spirit and still struggle with sin?

I guess that depends on what you mean by "struggling with sin"! If you are consistently giving in to sin, then the Holy Spirit can't be controlling or filling your life. But if you are asking, "Will I still commit sin after learning about the filling of the Holy Spirit?" — the answer is an emphatic *yes.*

You may find yourself committing sin and confessing it several times throughout the day. That's not spiritual weakness; it is evidence that you're living and breathing spiritually! Becoming aware of sin and dealing with it has been described as "spiritual breathing."

Spiritual breathing involves "exhaling": admitting your sin to the Lord as it occurs. You recognize that you have sinned and usurped the Lord's place as head of your life. By "exhaling," you are removing the impure, and you are claiming the forgiveness that is yours through Christ's death on the cross.

Spiritual breathing also includes "inhaling": asking God to again fill you with His Holy Spirit, to again be the head of your life. Remember that He doesn't leave you when you sin. But you have ignored His leading, and now you are once again following His direction. You are learning to trust Him, which takes time. Don't become discouraged when you fall into sin: Learn to get back up.

The youngest of our three children learned how to walk this past year. It took a while. She didn't wake up on her first birthday, vault over the rails of her crib and jog to a toddler aerobics class. Her first steps were tentative and wobbly. She fell into mud puddles, coffee tables and laundry baskets. But she never gave up. Eventually her steps turned into stronger, confident ones. She still falls down at times (and so do her parents!), but she gets back up.

We never become immune to sin; sinlessness is reserved for heaven. As chapter 10 will explain, we can learn to battle temptation, to *sin less.* But even then there will be occasions when we sin and need to breathe spiritually, whether we're in the first year of our Christian life or in our seventieth.

3. What if my life hasn't changed much yet?

Has it occurred to you that your level of spiritual growth may be exactly where God wants it? We've looked at two types of Christians, the carnal and the spiritual. But there is a third category of Christian: the new Christian. Remember what Paul told those Corinthians? "Brothers, I could not address you as spiritual but as worldly — mere infants in Christ."

Several years earlier, Paul had led many of those Corinthian believers to Christ. At that time he didn't expect them to be mature, spiritual believers. But instead of following a normal growth pattern of spiritual maturity for a Christian, the believers at Corinth became carnal. If you've only been a believer for a few months, you're still a "baby" Christian — not carnal, just young.

Each September when we lived in the midwest our family would head for Stover's Orchards in Three Rivers, Michigan. We knew we would be greeted by neatly labeled rows of apple trees. We filled bushel baskets with Mackintoshes, Winesaps and Romes.

Near the back of the orchard were rows of trees that were not laden with apples. In fact, they had no fruit at all. But they weren't dead; they were just young. Some had not yet reached five feet in height. While the older trees had matured and were bent over with apples, these young trees were just busy growing.

If you are obeying Christ today and trusting His power to change you, then you are exactly where God wants you to be. Don't agonize over the "fruit" you feel you lack. I never saw one of those young trees ever comparing itself with the older ones. Growth is a process, and each part of the process is vital.

I find that as I obey Christ and don't worry about comparing myself to other Christians, I enjoy being a Christian. Then I want to tell others about how they can become Christians too.

But let's save that topic for another chapter.

Growing Deeper...

1. Read John 14, 15 and 16. Jesus' discourse occurs during His final evening with the disciples before His crucifixion. Did the disciples understand what Jesus was teaching them?

2. Underline the word *obey* in these chapters. How often is the word *love* found in the same verses?

3. What does Jesus teach about prayer in these chapters? Why would He talk about prayer when He's teaching about the Holy Spirit?

Recommended Reading

The Secret: How to Live With Purpose and Power by Bill Bright (Here's Life Publishers). In an honest and easy-to-read manner, Bright presents the process of being filled with the Holy Spirit and shares how Christians can live in tune with God's supernatural purpose for their lives.

The Holy Spirit by Bill Bright (Here's Life Publishers). Subtitled "The Key to Supernatural Living," this book is a thorough and practical look at the role of the Holy Spirit.

Balancing the Christian Life by Charles Ryrie (Moody Press). Ryrie amplifies some biblical concepts regarding the Holy Spirit in relation to spiritual gifts, legalism and personal holiness.

Chapter 9

I Want to Tell My Friends!

You just never know, when you take the initiative
to share Christ, what will become of it.
—Bill Bright

Have you tried telling your family about your faith in Christ? How did they react? And how about your friends? Were they eager to hear about Christ — or eager to change the subject?

My own experience has been that some people are eager to accept Christ. Some reject Him. Most listen and decide to think about it later on their own.

Each of us as Christians wants to tell our friends and family about Christ. What could be more important than letting them know Him? In this chapter you will learn about sharing the good news with others: what to communicate, how to communicate it and how your life confirms your message.

After Jesus' resurrection, and shortly before His ascension into heaven, He gathered His followers on a mountain in Galilee, sixty miles away from the busy city life of Jerusalem. On a similar mountain less than three years earlier, He had selected each of them for that intimate circle of friends, the twelve disciples. During their years together they had seen Him teach large crowds on such mountainsides, watched Him feed multitudes and heal many. Now only Judas was gone.

What Jesus told them that day both startled and excited them:

> All authority in heaven and on earth has been given to me. Therefore go and make disciples of all nations, baptizing them in the name of the Father and of the Son and of the Holy Spirit, and teaching them to obey everything I have commanded you. And surely I will be with you always, to the very end of the age (Matthew 28:18-20, NIV).

Christ, instead of remaining on earth to spread His message via miracle and preaching, was leaving. The kingdom of God would spread through His disciples.

Why Witness?

As His disciple, your motivation for witnessing to others is obedience and compassion. Do you love Jesus? Obey Him. John 14:21 tells us: "Whoever has my commands and obeys them, he is the one who loves me" (NIV). "So we make it our goal," Paul said to the Corinthian Christians, "to please him, whether we are at home in the body or away from it" (2 Corinthians 5:9, NIV).

Witnessing is more than our responsibility — it's also our privilege. Bill Bright, founder of Campus Crusade for Christ, explains that the greatest experience in life is to become a Christian. After becoming a Christian, the greatest thing you can do for another person is to help them know Christ.

Compassion motivates you to witness as you remember what life was like for you without Christ.

Romans 10:13,14 says:

> Anyone who calls upon the name of the Lord will be
> saved. But how shall they ask him to save them unless
> they believe in him? And how can they believe in him if
> they have never heard about him? And how can they hear
> about him unless someone tells them?

But what do you say when you witness? Part of your
responsibility as His servant is to be sure that you communicate the gospel clearly. Learning the content of the
gospel and setting the context in which you communicate
it allows your witness to be more effective.

Content: Telling the Gospel Clearly

You may think: *I know what it means to be a Christian! Why bother with this?* There's a difference between
knowing what you have heard and how well you can explain
to others. Evangelist Paul Little compares it with a compli-
cated math problem. You listened to the professor's
explanation in class but found the whole thing too complex
when you attempted to explain it later to a friend.

So what *exactly* do you tell people about Jesus
Christ?

1. God loves them.

Each of us searches for significance and love. The
Bible teaches that we are not put here by chance. We are
not the product of impersonal evolutionary forces. Life has
far more meaning than the survival of the fittest. Someone
does care very deeply and understands our silent cry for
help. To help you communicate God's love, study these verses: John 3:16; Romans 5:8; Ephesians 2:4-7.

2. Man is sinful.

Part of telling people what Christ has done for them
means telling them that they are sinners. If man isn't lost,

he doesn't need to be saved. But we don't need to rub it in their faces—we are sinners too (Romans 3:23). By *sinfulness*, we aren't saying that man has no value or that he is incapable of good acts toward his fellow man. What we are saying is that none of those acts can earn a way to heaven. God doesn't weigh our bad works against our good works. We deserve separation from God for our sins, no matter what they are: "For the wages of sin is death . . ." (Romans 6:23).

3. Christ paid for their sin.

Why stress the death of Christ? Because without the death of Christ there would be no forgiveness of sins (Hebrews 7:27; 1 Peter 2:24). The message of God's love is incomplete until we couple it with God's justice. Christ bore the penalty for our sins (1 Timothy 1:15). His death wasn't just a demonstration of how much He loves us; it was a payment to satisfy God's justice. He told His disciples, "For even the Son of Man did not come to be served, but to serve, and to give his life as a ransom for many" (Mark 10:45, NIV).

4. Christ is God.

In order to pay for man's sin, Christ had to be both God and man (2 Corinthians 5:19; Colossians 1:19,20; 2:9). If Christ had been God without being man, God couldn't have identified with our humanity; if Christ had been mere man without being God, He couldn't have paid for the sins of all mankind. Christ, the God-man, took on our sins. As a result, He is the only way to God: "I am the way and the truth and the life. No one comes to the Father except through me" (John 14:6, NIV).

5. Christ was resurrected from the dead.

There is an additional element to the good news: Christ, who died on our behalf, is alive. Because of the resurrection of Christ, we celebrate an empty tomb. Without the resurrection, our faith would be worthless (1

Corinthians 15:13,14,17). Again we see the uniqueness of Jesus. He not only claimed to be God, but He also used the resurrection to show His deity and power over death (John 11:25; 1 Corinthians 15:55,56). We cannot have a personal relationship with Mohammed, Confucius or Buddha — they are all dead. But Jesus is alive today, and we can know Him.

6. We must respond by faith in order to have eternal life.

In salvation, I know that Jesus is God, that I am a sinner, that He died in payment for my sins, and then I accept His payment for my sins. That is what the Bible refers to as "believing in" or "receiving" Christ (John 1:12). I am accepting the gift of eternal life, which I have not earned and do not deserve, from a God who made us and chose to love us even though it cost Him His Son (Ephesians 2:8,9; Titus 3:5).

A Recommendation

One of the clearest means of presenting the gospel is through a booklet such as *Would You Like to Know God Personally.* (A copy of the text is in Appendix B.) This booklet is a revision of *The Four Spiritual Laws,* which has been used around the world to present Christ to millions.

Why use a booklet for talking about something as personal as your faith? I find that a booklet can be used either personally or impersonally. If used with genuine concern, it offers several advantages. It keeps the conversation centered on Christ rather than peripheral issues. It covers all of the elements of the gospel message. It brings the person you're talking with to a clear point of decision about Christ: He is asked where he is in relation to Christ, and where he would like to be. It also includes Scriptures that assure him of salvation.

There is a final advantage to using a booklet: The person you're sharing with can take it with him! Even the clearest gospel presentation may not be understood the first time it is heard, though many are ready to accept Christ the first time they hear the gospel. Giving a person something to read allows him to reconsider and invite Christ into his life later if he doesn't do so with you.

Context: How to Share the World's Greatest News

Be Authentic

When some Christians witness, their whole manner and tone of voice changes. They are at ease talking about the Yankees or how terrible the TV shows are this season, but they tense up when it comes to telling their neighbor that they have discovered a purpose in life through Christ. If you ever feel like this, be honest with the person you're talking to. Try saying, "You know, Christ has become really important to me and I would like to talk about it, but I am afraid that I might offend you."

Explain what God has done in your life, but try not to sound perfect. Some people think that if you're a Christian you'll hear voices and walk on water. Let others see that Christians are real people. Christians love sports, hate paying bills and end up with unmatched socks in the clothes dryer, just like everyone else.

Authenticity also means that your life confirms your message. People grow tired of phoniness. The apostle Paul said to the Thessalonians that they not only *heard* his message but they *saw* how his life was further proof of the truth of his message (1 Thessalonians 1:5; 2:8). The message of his life did not contradict the message of his mouth.

I was a young Christian when an economics teacher asked class members to explain their purpose in life. He seemed pleased by several students who half-jokingly said they wanted high salaries and everything money could buy.

He scoffed at replies that were more altruistic. Then he stopped in front of my desk. "What is your purpose in life?" he asked.

"To glorify God," I replied. He paused momentarily.

"Well, Mr. Pogue," he said, "we will have to put you under glass."

Letting others know you are a Christian will subject your life to close scrutiny. It's as if you've announced your candidacy for President of the United States: Suddenly people are very interested in how you live your public and private life. But what a great opportunity to show that Christianity is more than just talk!

Confirming your witness through your life doesn't replace your verbal witnessing, though. Both are needed. You cannot just live a Christian life and hope that others will notice; they may notice that you live a good life, but they won't know why. Jesus lived a perfect life *and* He was constantly proclaiming the gospel. Jesus' command is to witness by word and deed.

Leave the Results to the Holy Spirit

Seminars on witnessing taught by Campus Crusade for Christ always stress reliance upon the Holy Spirit. They emphasize this phrase:

> Successful witnessing is taking the initiative
> to share Christ in the power of the Holy Spirit
> and leaving the results to God.

Relying upon the power of the Holy Spirit in witnessing means believing that He will lead your conversation even as you use your mental and verbal skills in presenting the gospel to others. The results are up to God. Don't get confused about whose job it is to save people!

Saving people is God's responsibility; your responsibility is to present the gospel.

Be a Listener

A year after becoming a Christian, I attended a weekend workshop where I learned how I could witness to others. Soon afterwards I was taking an advanced algebra class in high school and decided that I should witness to Steve Sturm. It wasn't that I thought Steve needed Christ; in fact, of all the people in that class I felt he was the one who was most likely to be a Christian. I just wanted to witness to someone who was on my side!

One morning both Steve and I arrived a few minutes before class. With a lump in my throat I pulled out a copy of the *Four Spiritual Laws,* thrust it into his hand and asked him if he was a Christian. Steve replied that he was. My heart stopped racing. I had witnessed to a fellow student and lived to tell about it.

My problem? I had seen witnessing as an *event* rather than a *conversation* with a person. Since then I have learned that a lot of witnessing involves asking questions and listening. I want to know what the people I'm talking with think. So I may ask, "How do you think a person becomes a Christian?" or "Why should God allow you into heaven?"

Stick With Them

Being authentic and learning to listen will enhance your witness if you combine it with one very important quality: a commitment to stick with the people you witness to. Try to view witnessing more as a process than a one-time shot. Of course there will be times when you will have only a few minutes with a stranger, such as on an airplane or in a grocery store. But most of your witnessing will occur in the context of relationships.

Think of the people who compose your world: those

people you *thought* about sending Christmas cards to last year; your acquaintances at work, on the softball team or in aerobics class; your relatives you see on holidays; the guys at your car dealer's service department who know you on a first-name basis because your car keeps breaking down. This is your world, and many of those in your world may get to hear about Christ because of you!

Sticking with people means remaining their friend after you've witnessed to them the first time. It even means remaining close by to help out after they accept Christ. Paul explains: "So everywhere we go, we talk about Christ to all who will listen, warning them and teaching them as well as we know how. We want to be able to present each one to God, perfect because of what Christ has done for each of them" (Colossians 1:28).

Expect God to Use You

Remember my first attempt at witnessing in algebra class? After discovering that Steve Sturm was a fellow believer, we became friends, although we lost contact with each other during our college years. After I graduated I found out he had become an architect and was working in our hometown. I stopped by his office, where he was hunched over his drafting board.

After a few minutes of catching up on our lives, Steve said, "You probably don't remember this, but one time in high school you showed me a *Four Spiritual Laws* booklet and asked me if I was a Christian."

I told him I remembered.

"You know, it really bothered me that someone had to ask me if I was a Christian," he continued. "I decided when I went to college that I would become involved with the Navigators, a student Christian group, and really grow in my faith. I wanted to become the one asking others about their faith. God really used your witness that day back in high school in my life."

As you communicate your faith in Christ to others, don't be surprised at how God is able to use you! The Christian life isn't a humdrum religious ritual; it's a living relationship. But it's also a battle. We'll look at that in the next chapter.

Growing Deeper...

1. Make a list of five people you would like to talk with about Christ. Pray for them for a week and see what opportunities God opens up.

2. Read John 18 and 19. How does Jesus respond to His accusers? Who were they? How does Peter respond to his accusers? Who were they? Some skeptics of Christianity have argued for a "swoon theory" of Jesus' death: that Jesus did not die but only swooned or fainted. What evidence do you find in chapter 19 of John to refute that theory?

Recommended Reading

Witnessing Without Fear by Bill Bright (Here's Life Publishers). Though Bright has witnessed for more than thirty years, he still describes himself as a shy person. Learn how he overcame his own fears and how God may use your witness.

How to Give Away Your Faith by Paul Little (Inter-Varsity Press). Little communicates clearly and convincingly what it means to tell others about Christ, as well as how to consistently live out the faith you profess.

Tell It Often, Tell It Well by Mark McCloskey (Here's Life Publishers). McCloskey provides a thorough explanation of what the gospel message is, as well as how to make your witnessing "others-centered."

Chapter 10

Preparation for Hard Times

When the going gets tough,
the tough use Scripture.

The Bible places great importance on your mind. "You were taught," the apostle Paul told his Christian friends, "to be made new in the attitude of your minds" (Ephesians 4:22,23, NIV). "Do not conform any longer to the pattern of this world, but be transformed by the renewing of your mind . . . ," he wrote another church (Romans 12:2, NIV).

You want to serve Christ. But it's hard sometimes when your life — especially your *thought* life — isn't consistent with Christianity. You can't watch TV, drive to work tomorrow or sit through lunch with co-workers without being bombarded with messages that contradict or ridicule your faith. Your mind can be taken hostage by those thoughts.

The Bible also talks about your desires and will, referring to them as your heart. The greatest commandment is to love the Lord with all your heart. Where your heart is, there your treasure is, Jesus explained. Paul wrote, ". . . set your hearts on things above . . . not on

96

earthly things" (Colossians 3:1,2, NIV).

Yet you may find yourself echoing the words of the prophet Jeremiah: "The heart is deceitful above all things and beyond cure. Who can understand it?" (Jeremiah 17:9, NIV)

God has given you a means of purifying your mind and of changing your heart. He has given you the Bible. It's effect in your life is increased when you memorize it.

Jesus was tempted by Satan after fasting in the desert for forty days. Jesus rebuked Satan each time He was tempted by quoting from the book of Deuteronomy. He said, "It is written: 'Man does not live on bread alone, but on every word that comes from the mouth of God' " (Matthew 4:4, NIV).

Two verses I've memorized have been an island of spiritual refuge when I have faced temptation: "How can a young man keep his way pure? By living according to your word . . . . I have hidden your word in my heart that I might not sin against you" (Psalm 119:9,11, NIV). I can't qualify as the young man anymore, but I sure can identify with his desire to stay pure. Jesus prayed for His disciples: "Make them pure and holy through teaching them your words of truth" (John 17:17). By memorizing Scriptures you transform your thinking and focus on the right things in the midst of temptation.

Bible memorization. You may envision a squinty-eyed scholar hidden in the recesses of a seminary, or a child reciting verses learned by rote. Put aside these ideas. Scripture memory is vital to your spiritual growth. But it may sound beyond reach — you're too busy or too old for much memorization of anything. Or are you?

Sometimes we get nudged out of our prejudices by an event that awakens us to the truth. That's what happened to Roy Robertson. He had become a Christian early in childhood, attended church regularly and went to Christian meetings in college. Yet, he admits, he never took knowing the Bible too seriously. One Sunday morning changed all that.

Robertson was gunnery officer aboard the U.S.S. Vega on that Sunday morning of December 7, 1941, when Japanese torpedo bombers attacked Battleship Row in nearby Pearl Harbor. The Vega was not exactly a primary target of the Japanese during their attack. She was a World War I vintage supply ship berthed in nearby Honolulu Harbor and was spared the brunt of the Japanese bombers. That was of little help.

The surprise attack created confusion among the Vega's crew. All of the live ammunition was padlocked inside the ship's hold, and no one could open it. After a frantic debate, a blowtorch was used to cut open the hold and ammunition was loaded. But for the first thirty-one minutes of the attack, the ship's guns fired only dummy rounds at enemy planes.

Robertson afterward thought a lot about those thirty-one minutes. He saw a parallel to his spiritual life. The night before Pearl had been attacked, Robertson had attended a small group Bible study where he met men and women who were serious about knowing Christ and could quote Bible verses from memory. Around them, he felt as unprepared for living the Christian life consistently as he did when he faced the Japanese that next morning. He had been firing dummy rounds instead of God's living Word.

The key to spiritual preparation, Robertson decided, was to systematically learn God's Word. In the next five years he memorized 1,800 Bible verses and saw his Christian life revolutionized. He has used what he learned for more than forty years as a missionary in China, Singapore and Malaysia. There he has taught hundreds of new Christians about spiritual growth. *And* Scripture memorization.

The Key to Memorization

When you think of actually memorizing, you may ask yourself, "How can I memorize verses when I have such a terrible memory?"

Psychologist Tim LaHaye explains that our apprehension about memorization is not so much from a mental block as it is with an ambition block: "If I were to ask for your address or phone number, you would have no trouble recalling it. Anyone that can do that can memorize Bible verses. Very honestly, memorization involves hard work but it pays greater dividends to your spiritual life than any other known method of Bible study."[1]

All of us can memorize Scripture. Some may memorize faster than others, but we are all capable of memorization.

The key motivation for memorizing Scripture is realizing how important it really is. I hope it won't take a squadron of torpedo bombers to awaken you to this. Perhaps just understanding what the Bible says about memorizing will be sufficient!

Why Memorize?

Psalm 1 describes the person who memorizes God's Word and then thinks about it often (meditates upon it):

> Oh, the joys of those who do not follow evil men's advice, who do not hang around with sinners, scoffing at the things of God: But they delight in doing everything God wants them to, and day and night are always meditating on his laws and thinking about ways to follow him more closely (Psalm 1:1,2).

When you care enough about knowing God's Word to memorize it, it becomes a part of your thoughts. You find yourself suddenly remembering it throughout the day. If you awaken at night full of anger or fear, you can choose to mentally review verses in God's Word that deal with those emotions.

The psalmist explains the result in a person's life because of such meditation: "They are like trees along a river bank bearing luscious fruit each season without fail. Their leaves shall never wither, and all they do shall prosper" (Psalm 1:3). Those who meditate upon God's Word keep going when the going gets tough. They don't wilt under pressure. They are consistent.

Jesus exemplified that consistency in His life. We can't claim to live exactly as the sinless, incarnate God did, but we can value what He valued. Pick up any of the Gospels and begin reading about Jesus. He is often quoting Scripture—from memory! Nearly 10 percent of the words of Jesus in the Gospels are quotations from the Old Testament. By having Scripture memorized, Jesus could use the right Scripture for the need of the moment, like a craftsman who instinctively reaches for the right tool. The same can occur in your life.

Romans 12:2 says, "Do not conform any longer to the pattern of this world, but be transformed by the renewing of your mind. Then you will be able to test and approve what God's will is—his good, pleasing and perfect will" (NIV). Memorizing Scripture and then consciously thinking about it gives you a grid with which to evaluate all the messages you receive from advertising, friends at work, your family . . . everything you are exposed to. Instead of remaining conformed to the world, you are transformed as God's Word renews your mind.

How to Memorize

Let's get started. Look at your watch and note the time. What follows will require some effort, but you will be surprised by how little time it actually takes to memorize a verse or two letter perfect. (Even those who have memorized thousands of verses began by memorizing one verse at a time.) Let's try Philippians 4:6,7:

> Do not be anxious about anything, but in every-thing, by prayer and petition, with thanksgiving, present your requests to God. And the peace of God, which transcends all understanding, will guard your hearts and your minds in Christ Jesus (NIV).

Memorization begins first with *familiarization.* Read the verses aloud several times. This involves your mind in three ways: seeing, speaking and hearing. Next, copy the verses down on a 3x5 card or a large self-stick type note. By writing the verses on a note card you will have a handy reminder to place on the refrigerator or the bathroom mirror.

Carefully compare your own copy with the version in this book. You may be surprised to find that you omitted or added a word in copying the verses!

Now try quoting the verses from memory. Don't feel bad if you have to stop and look at your card for help. Just keep going phrase by phrase. Once you feel like you have the verses memorized, write the verses out from memory.

Finished? Look at your watch again. You are thir-ty-nine words—two verses—closer to being a consistent memorizer.

Amplification

Amplification involves gaining the fullest meaning from the text. This involves looking up definitions to words that aren't totally clear, as well as reading the verses in their context to determine meaning. You may have been hindered in memorizing Philippians 4:6,7 because you didn't entirely understand what the verses were saying. In particular, the meaning of several of the words may be unclear. What does it mean to *petition* God? And what does *transcend* mean?

Webster's Dictionary reveals that *petition* is an earnest request, with a second meaning of a formal request made to a superior. *Transcend* means "to rise above or go beyond the limits of."

Philippians 4:6,7 is saying that if you present your request to God, who is your superior, He gives you His peace. It becomes God's job to worry about your problem! That does not free you from personal responsibility, but it does free you from personal anxiety. You still have to work through the problem, but the worry is given to God.

Personalization

Personalization applies the verse to your own situation. Consider how Philippians 4:6,7 applies to you:

> "I will not be anxious about anything, but in everything by prayer and petition with thanksgiving, I will present my requests to God. And I know that the peace of God, which transcends all understanding, will guard my heart and my mind in Christ Jesus."

Writing and thinking about how this verse applies to you allows God's Word to change patterns in your life. When you become fearful or sense a lot of stress, tell God your problems. These needs are presented with thanksgiving and the confidence that God's peace will guard your thinking.

To make it even more personal, you might write out, "What situations cause me to be anxious?" and then list specific situations or areas that make you stressful. Include the things that make you lie awake at night or wake you early in the morning with a tight knot in your stomach. Decide to pray over these things, recalling that prayer is not limited to "spiritual" areas, but includes talking to God about the money you need to get the car fixed or your kid's problems at school.

Review

It will not help much to memorize these verses today, only to forget them tomorrow. The key to effective memorization is review. Putting your memory verses on 3x5 cards allows you to place them in a file box for review. Here is one method of review that many have found helpful:

Review once a day for seven days;
     once a week for seven weeks;
     once a month for seven months.

I hope you will set aside time today to begin memorizing and meditating on Scripture. The first week will be the hardest, but also the most important. You'll begin to learn firsthand the value of this practice.

Francis Cosgrove Jr., like Roy Robertson, has memorized Scripture extensively. He gives this encouragement:

Why do I memorize Scripture? Because I have convictions about it. I know God wants me to know His Word, and He wants me to share it with others, so I discipline myself to add more verses to my biblical vocabulary. I keep adding verses, but I remember that there was a day when I had only one verse memorized.[2]

Of course, Scripture memory alone won't guarantee a healthy, growing spiritual life, but it does provide a powerful resource when you're tempted. Yet, even with this tool, you still need to live a life of total dependence on God. And, as we will see in the next chapter, you really can't live the Christian life — even with memorized verses — in isolation.

Growing Deeper...

1. Here's a suggested list of verses to help you get started with your Scripture memorization:

- 1 Corinthians 10:13
- 1 John 1:9
- 1 John 5:11-13
- Romans 3:23
- John 1:12
- Romans 5:8
- Ephesians 2:8,9
- Galatians 2:20
- Philippians 4:13
- Romans 12:1,2
- Romans 8:28
- John 16:33
- Ephesians 6:10,11
- 1 Peter 5:7
- Acts 1:8

2. Read John chapters 20 and 21. What are the reactions of the disciples to Jesus' resurrection? Was His resurrection physical, or simply imaginary? In conclusion, what have you learned from your reading of John's Gospel?

Recommended Reading

Topical Memory System by Navpress. This inexpensive series provides you with the verse cards for memorizing as well as suggestions for being consistent in Scripture memory.

Chapter 11

Your Lifeline

*No man is an island, entire of itself; every man is
a piece of the continent, part of the main.*
—*John Donne, Meditation XVII*

Wouldn't it be great to know older Christians who can help you grow in your faith? Christians who listen to your doubts, who understand your problems? Who model a life of faith and dependence on God?

The apostle Paul and his co-workers played such a supportive role to new Christians in the ancient city of Thessalonica. Paul later reminded them, "For you know that we dealt with each of you as a father deals with his own children, encouraging, comforting and urging you to live lives worthy of God, who calls you into his kingdom and glory" (1 Thessalonians 2:11,12, NIV).

Is there someone like that in your life now?

Charles W. Colson, special counsel to former President Nixon, became a Christian less than a year before entering federal prison for his involvement in the Watergate scandal. In the months preceding his trial in Washington, Colson began to discover a network of Christians that crossed political lines. Men would drop by his office, pray with him and tell him that they were there to help. One former politician later offered to take Colson's place in jail.

Those older Christians were helping Colson make the transition from his old life to his new life in Christ. It was not easy, as Colson discovered: "In the days which followed I learned how hard it is for a new Christian to turn himself over to God completely. Daily prayer and a study of Scripture helped, but the old self keeps fighting; the old ego and pride die hard."[1]

In the months following Colson's indictment and conviction, Christians continued to stand by his side. His new brothers in Christ visited him in prison, praying with him, reading the Bible and showing love and concern. These weren't prison chaplains on counseling rounds—they were busy career people. But they were also new Christian friends who cared. Colson wrote to one such friend, "I can't tell you how much these visits have meant to me. I often feel like I am on a lonely frontier away from the spiritual home of our fellowship."[2]

The moment you began your relationship with Jesus Christ you also began a relationship with other Christians. Now you are part of God's family, and in God's family there are no orphans. God did not intend for His children to live as individual islands of faith, but rather as a community of believers, interrelated with each other and part of something much bigger than themselves.

That "something" is the Church.

Our English word *church* comes from a Greek word meaning "belonging to the Lord." The Bible explains that every Christian—every true believer in Jesus Christ—is a part of the Church even if they've never stepped inside a church building. God's universal Church (usually spelled with a capital "C") crosses denominational, cultural and national lines. The Bible refers to this union of believers as "the body of Christ."

It was the body of Christ that ministered to Charles Colson: Christians from many different churches and denominations. There were differences in how they worshiped on Sunday morning, but each of them loved God and loved God's family. You are family with Christians everywhere! That is the universal aspect to the Church.

You are also family with believers right where you live. They are waiting to meet you — in a local church.

At this point you may be thinking, *Great! But how do I pick a church? There are so many denominations — it's all so confusing!*

How do you find the right church for you?

The "Perfect Church"

As a new Christian in high school I was very critical of churches. Why weren't they doing a better job of teaching the Bible, of reaching the world for Christ? Why were there so many hypocrites? I knew that when I became an adult I would either find or start a church that was really "doing something."

One Sunday morning the minister at my parents' church spoke about the role of the church. I only remember one statement from the entire sermon: "If you ever find a perfect church, don't join it. You'll ruin it, because you are an imperfect person." I realized that I was putting my own church and every other church under terrific scrutiny, asking them to reach standards that I could not even reach myself. I'm not perfect — so why should my church be?

The church is God's institution. Christ established it as the earthly representative of Himself. It is inhabited by people who are still in the process of becoming mature in Christ. Some people in the churches you visit may not even be Christians, or if they are, they have placed other priorities in life higher than Christ.

While you won't be able to find a perfect church, you should be able to find one that is perfect for you. How? By asking these questions as you visit churches:

1. Does the church demonstrate love?

Christians are to be known for their love. Jesus said, "As I have loved you, so you must love one another. By this all men will know that you are my disciples, if you love one another" (John 13:34,35, NIV). Consequently, as Francis Schaeffer observes, "If I am not showing love, the world has a right to judge me as not being a Christian." So how do you know if a church is demonstrating love?

Gene Getz, in *The Measure of a Church*, says that biblical love is like Christlikeness: "Biblical love involves demonstrating those attitudes and actions toward others that Christ demonstrated when He came into the world and lived among men."[3]

Such love is fleshed out in equality rather than favoritism and prejudice; in forgiveness and encouragement rather than bitterness and gossip; in patience and understanding with the unlovely person.

A church member — me — was moving, and other members loaded a truck when the temperature was 10 degrees below zero. I will never forget that demonstration of love. Another church member needed an expensive surgery and faced a long recovery. Members of our church gave money anonymously, stayed at the hospital during the operation, and provided meals and services to the family for weeks.

At one Sunday evening service in another church, I watched an engaged couple confess their sin of premarital sex with its resulting pregnancy. They asked for the church's forgiveness and help. The church gave both. They supported those teenagers, who were soon to be parents, with genuine love.

When you see love demonstrated in a church, you are seeing Christ at work.

2. How does the church use the Bible?

Nearly every worship service will include a time when the minister reads a Bible passage and expounds upon it. As you listen to his message, keep a mental or written outline. Does he teach you what the passage is about, or does he use it as a springboard for his own arguments? You ought to think afterward, *Now I understand what this Bible passage means.*

As you meet church members, find out ways in which they are being equipped for ministry. Some churches do a tremendous job of teaching their members how to study the Bible, how to counsel friends, how to care for the aged and homeless, how to share their faith.

Are the members being equipped to study God's Word and live it out in service to others? If so, they are fulfilling one of the primary functions of the local church: equipping (Ephesians 4:11-13).

Find out what the church believes. They probably have a printed copy of their statement of faith. Read over it, and make sure you understand it and agree with it. If you have questions about its beliefs, ask a pastor.

3. What does the minister talk about?

Many ministers do not consider themselves great personal evangelists, but even so, they ought to be talking to people about Christ. You should be able to ask a pastor, "Who are you currently witnessing to and praying for?" And the minister (or someone he has trained) should be able to take you with him and demonstrate how he communicates his faith to others.

I have spent time with some ministers who are gifted Bible teachers and some who are very effective witnesses for Christ. Others are only of average abilities and gifts, yet their genuine love for Christ is evident. I find that I learn a lot from each.

If you are seriously considering becoming a member of the church, make an appointment to talk with the minister. Ask, "Could you share with me what you see as the overall goals or direction of the church? I want to know how I can be involved." Communicate that you are not judging the church, but that you want to be a part of the church to give and serve, and not just for what the church offers you.

4. What do the members talk about?

We all need time to talk about yesterday's ball game or how our kids are doing. It's not unspiritual to want to share a wide variety of topics with other Christians. Christians should enjoy life! Forget the straight-laced, sober and sad look.

But — if the conversations in the church are no different than the conversations at work, something is missing. Jesus Christ is the most wonderful person in the universe. When we spend time with other people who have discovered this, we will want to talk about Him.

After you've visited a number of churches and narrowed your choices down, go to programs beyond the Sunday morning services. Attend midweek services, home Bible studies, church dinners and softball games. Look for opportunities to get to know the other members as people.

Good churches may seem cold at first, but they are often full of caring people. Many churches are constantly changing membership as people move in and out of the city. Some members may be reluctant to introduce themselves because they are fairly new to the church too. Take the initiative in getting to know people.

Commit Yourself

You may not intend to avoid finding a church, but it's easy to prolong the process. If you are new in a city, it will take time to find a church. Set a reasonable deadline, and then commit to a church. Don't get in the habit of saying, "I'm attending First Church, but I'm not really happy there so I may look for another one sometime."

Commitment to a church, like a marriage, takes work. It will not always be fun. If you are a person who is naturally analytical, be careful of being overly critical of a church and its members — you'll miss the blessing God has for you in His body. You can easily overestimate the strength of your own spiritual life if you continually compare it to others, opening yourself up to spiritual defeat by Satan.

Belgium during World War II overestimated its own strength. When Poland was invaded by Hitler in 1939, England and France pledged their aid and entered the war. Neighboring Belgium opted for neutrality, insisting that it wanted no pretense for German invasion of its own soil.

Part of Belgium's recalcitrance was due to its belief in its defenses. A string of large fortresses lined its border, with Eben Emael being its trump. This huge garrison of 1200 men was perched high above the countryside on the country's southeastern border and was considered impregnable.

In the predawn hours of May 10, 1940, German commandos landed on the roof of the garrison, dynamiting artillery pieces, observation towers, ventilator shafts and exits. The Belgian soldiers who were confidently asleep in their fortress were now prisoners. The Belgian commander of Eben Emael frantically appealed for help. The nearest forts responded by shelling it.

Weeks later the king of Belgium surrendered to the

Germans without warning. Suddenly the 300,000 French and British troops who had belatedly enlisted to reinforce the Belgians were now nearly encircled by the Germans.

With the Germans threatening a final advance and with the sea at their backs, the Allies fought in the hope of rescue. Their only hope of escape from wholesale slaughter rested upon the bomb-pitted docks of a tiny seaport—Dunkirk.

A withdrawal of that size would take the already hard-pressed British navy weeks to accomplish. "Operation Dynamo" took only nine days.

Nearly 900 vessels—civilian vessels— sailed from England to the smoke-shrouded port. The Royal Navy and Air Force provided a wall of antiaircraft and artillery fire as fishing boats, yachts, passenger steamers and tugboats shuttled troops across the English Channel.

The small craft sometimes listed heavily, but the flotilla never quit. In nine days those freshly appointed captains of the sea had rescued 338,000 men. Winston Churchill called it "a miracle of deliverance."

Christendom is littered with the remains of Christians who suffered a fate similar to Eben Emael, guided by the illusion that they are spiritually independent and strong. As we will see in the next chapter, we face a crafty enemy who exploits our independence.

You will not mature in your relationship with Christ isolated in a cocoon of private Christianity. There is a vast group of people who really care for you and will endure a lot to help you make it through tough times. They form God's own "miracle of deliverance." They form the church.

Growing Deeper...

Read the book of Ephesians, the tenth book in the New Testament.

1. What does it teach about the church?

2. Underline each occurrence of the phrase "in Christ." What has God given you personally, and the church collectively, in Christ?

3. Notice each usage of "live a life of." Ephesians has been called the book of Christian living. What values and behavior are to characterize your life and the life of the church?

Chapter 12

The Adventure
Up the Road

But grow in spiritual strength and become
better acquainted with our Lord
and Savior Jesus Christ.
(2 Peter 3:18)

You have come far in such a short time. You know who Christ is and why He died. You know who you are in Christ. You can study His Word and live by His Spirit. You know how to pray and how to communicate your faith in Christ to others. Ahead is a great adventure of living with Christ.

The book of Hebrews says of the Christian life: "Let us run with patience the particular race that God has set before us" (Hebrews 12:2). The Christian life is an endurance race, an ultramarathon where finishing is more important than winning. The great adventures up the road come as you stay consistent in following Christ, as you "run with patience."

No one can predict what your particular race will include. God may give you health and wealth. He may give you sickness and poverty. He only promises that He will meet every need. That may involve peace of mind about your financial portfolio, or grace to endure another round of chemotherapy treatments that leave you nauseous and deeper in debt.

Can I take a minute to give you a caution and a conclusion? Far too many believers start out filled with good intentions, only to fade into complacency. I would like to see you stay strong in your relationship with Christ.

Dropping Like Flies

Bill Cosby tells of an episode at the end of his Army medic training that rudely awakened him to the realities of war. During their training the young recruits had their fears allayed about battlefield work by the fact that medics are protected by the Geneva Convention. Since no enemy would shoot him, a medic would not need a gun.

The final day of their training the medics were shown an actual battle film. To their horror they watched as medics, along with infantrymen, were dropping like flies in the face of enemy fire. The enemy they would actually be facing, their instructor solemnly told them, did not adhere to the Geneva Convention.

You face an enemy in your Christian life, and it is important for you to know that he adheres to no agreement! He is called Satan (meaning "accuser"). He is also referred to as the devil, the father of lies, the old serpent, the prince of the power of darkness, the wicked one, the tempter. Though the Bible does not provide much information about the origin of Satan, he apparently was the first creature made by God. Given great power, he also developed great pride and led a number of angels in rebellion against God. (You may want to read Revelation 12:7-10 for a description of this.)

There are two common mistakes you can make when you think about Satan. The first is to ignore him; the second is to focus on him.

Don't discount the reality of Satan. Satan does not appear in a red leotard with horns. He appears as an angel of light, a spiritual counterfeiter. He attempts to get you to doubt God's Word and pursue what you think is best.

He wants to thwart God's plans by getting you out of God's will. The Bible says: "Be self-controlled and alert. Your enemy the devil prowls around like a roaring lion looking for someone to devour" (1 Peter 5:8, NIV). He wants you to stop reading your Bible (or at least stop applying it). He wants to discourage you in prayer. He wants you to believe that immorality is satisfying and that holiness is prudish and boring. He wants you to use the ends to justify the means. He wants you to march to his tune while you imagine yourself free of his influence. Beware.

The second error is to be preoccupied with Satan. You begin to blame Satan rather than yourself for every unpleasant circumstance. Satan becomes the unseen hand behind your sinus cold, the dead car battery or your weight problem.

Don't give Satan too much credit for your sin either. Satan will tempt you, but he cannot force you into sin. You can't say, "The devil made me do it." Sin is your own choice.

Defeating Satan

The Bible is full of promises regarding God's power over Satan. John told new believers that there would be evil spirits in the world, but that Christians were not to worry: "You, dear children, are from God and have overcome [the evil spirits], because the one who is in you is greater than the one who is in the world" (1 John 4:4, NIV).

Since Satan is a spirit, he is overcome by spiritual means: "Last of all I want to remind you that your strength must come from the Lord's mighty power within you. Put on all of God's armor so that you will be able to stand safe against all strategies and tricks of Satan" (Ephesians 6:10,11). Just as you cannot live the Christian life without the Holy Spirit, you cannot overcome Satan's influence in your life without God's power. Claim His power and review these verses when you sense that Satan is attacking you.

Why all the caution about Satan? The greatest danger in the next year of your Christian life won't come from a direct assault on your new beliefs; it will come from the lie that there is a better road somewhere else. The apostle Paul told the Christians in Corinth:

> I am anxious for you with the deep concern of God himself—anxious that your love should be for Christ alone, just as a pure maiden saves her love for one man only, for the one who will be her husband. But I am frightened, fearing that in some way you will be led away from your pure and simple devotion to our Lord, just as Eve was deceived by Satan in the Garden of Eden (2 Corinthians 11:2,3).

Ever so subtly you are led away from a pure and simple devotion to Christ into a "less fanatical" view of religion. Your friends and family may call it a maturing process. Perhaps you will suddenly discover a "meaningful and intimate" but adulterous relationship or an opportunity for career advancement if you'll only compromise a bit on your "narrow" standards.

I hope not! You may swear that no one can knock you off the road of following Christ by force, but it won't take an army to defeat you—just a few "suggestions" to make you drift off course. And the sober truth is that you *will* drift off unless you make a deliberate choice to stay on track.

An Appetite for God

Over the past several years I have asked many

young, growing Christians to explain their greatest need. Their answers vary somewhat, but one response keeps coming up: "I want to know Christ better." The apostle Paul would have agreed with them. He said:

> . . . I consider everything a loss compared to the surpassing greatness of knowing Christ Jesus my Lord, for whose sake I have lost all things . . . . I want to know Christ and the power of his resurrection and the fellowship of sharing in his sufferings, becoming like him in his death, and so, somehow, to attain to the resurrection from the dead (Philippians 3:8-11, NIV).

The apostle Paul didn't quit the race, even though he had plenty of reasons to. He had been ridiculed, beaten and scourged, shipwrecked, deserted and slandered. What made Paul hang on?

It wasn't Paul's background, conversion experience or even his Christian service that set him apart. J. Dwight Pentecost explains Paul's tenacity: "He had an appetite for the person of Christ . . . . [A] desire to enter into a deep, personal, intimate, experiential knowledge of the Lord Jesus Christ."[1] Paul was not content to be casually acquainted with Christ; Christ had to be everything to him. Most of us do not know anything that well.

I have seen the Mississippi River several times, but I do not know her as Samuel Clemens and his colleagues did. Clemens was a steamboat pilot for a number of years before he became famous as Mark Twain. Navigating the silt-laden Mississippi with her ever-changing channels was a difficult enough task in the daylight. Night travel should have been unthinkable. Darkness obscured all of the familiar landmarks. Even the moonlight became a deceiver with its strange shadows. Yet nighttime navigation was standard procedure in the river pilot's work.

Early in his apprenticeship Clemens despaired of ever mastering night navigation. He considered quitting.

His master pilot explained the secret of such navigation: "You learn [the river] with such absolute certainty that you can always steer by the shape that's *in your head*, and never mind the one that's before your eyes."[2]

You don't just know *about* Jesus; you know *Him* — not casually, but deeply. Clemens could say, "The river is my life." The apostle Paul wrote, "Christ is my life." Is He becoming your life?

Stay strong in your relationship with Christ. Be a finisher and not just a starter with good intentions. A passage in the book of Hebrews that talks about the race of faith is followed by these words: "Let us fix our eyes on Jesus, the author and perfecter of our faith, who for the joy set before him endured the cross, scorning its shame, and sat down at the right hand of the throne of God" (Hebrews 12:2, NIV).

Like Clemens, you may consider quitting, but there's so much more to know! Take a lesson from something your dad probably told you as a kid. Remember those long days in the car when you were going to a relatives' place or on a family vacation? Thirty minutes out of the driveway you asked THE question: "Are we there yet?" Dad's reply was truthful, but unsatisfying: "We're not there yet, but we're getting closer."

Your Christian life may not be where you want it to be right now, but you're getting closer. Remember that Danish proverb back in chapter one? "The next mile is the only one a person really has to make." The adventure up the road continues for a lifetime—one mile at a time.

Appendix A

A Schedule of Bible Reading

Because the Bible is not arranged chronologically, and because the Old Testament is properly understood through the New Testament, I have included this schedule for reading the Bible. This particular order is designed to give you a good understanding of the major themes of Scripture and to acquaint you with much of its history.

- John
- 1 John
- Romans
- Galatians
- Ephesians
- Philippians
- Colossians
- Luke
- Acts
- 1 Thessalonians
- 2 Thessalonians
- 1 Timothy
- 2 Timothy
- James
- Mark
- 1 Corinthians
- 2 Corinthians
- Genesis
- Exodus
- Joshua
- Proverbs
- 1 Samuel
- 2 Samuel

Would You Like
to Know God Personally?

The following four principles will help you discover how to know God personally and experience the abundant life He promised.

1 GOD **LOVES** YOU AND CREATED YOU TO KNOW HIM PERSONALLY.

(References contained in these pages should be read in context from the Bible whenever possible.)

God's Love

"For God so loved the world, that He gave His only begotten Son, that whoever believes in Him should not perish, but have eternal life" (John 3:16).

God's Plan

"Now this is eternal life: that they may know you, the only true God, and Jesus Christ, whom you have sent" (John 17:3, NIV).

What prevents us from knowing God personally?

2 MAN IS **SINFUL** AND **SEPARATED** FROM GOD, SO WE CANNOT KNOW HIM PERSONALLY OR EXPERIENCE HIS LOVE.

Man Is Sinful

"For all have sinned and fall short of the glory of God" (Romans 3:23).

Man was created to have fellowship with God; but, because of his stubborn self-will, he chose to go his own independent way, and fellowship with God was broken. This self-will, characterized by an attitude of active rebellion or passive indifference, is evidence of what the Bible calls sin.

Man Is Separated

"For the wages of sin is death" (spiritual separation from God) (Romans 6:23).

HOLY GOD

SINFUL MAN

This diagram illustrates that God is holy and man is sinful. A great gulf separates the two. The arrows illustrate that man is continually trying to reach God and establish a personal relationship with Him through his own efforts, such as a good life, philosophy or religion.

The third principle explains the only way to bridge this gulf . . .

3 JESUS CHRIST IS GOD'S **ONLY** PROVISION FOR MAN'S SIN. THROUGH HIM ALONE WE CAN KNOW GOD PERSONAL-LY AND EXPERIENCE HIS LOVE.

He Died in Our Place

"But God demonstrates His own love toward us, in that while we were yet sinners, Christ died for us" (Romans 5:8).

He Rose From the Dead

"Christ died for our sins . . . He was buried . . . He was raised on the third day, accord-ing to the Scriptures . . . He appeared to Peter, then to the twelve. After that He ap-peared to more than five hundred" (1 Corin-thians 15:3-6).

He Is the Only Way to God

"Jesus said to him, 'I am the way, and the truth, and the life; no one comes to the Father, but through Me' " (John 14:6).

This diagram il-lustrates that God has bridged the gulf which separates us from Him by sending His Son, Jesus Christ, to die on the cross in our place to pay the penalty for our sins.

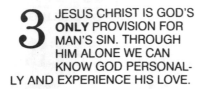

It is not enough just to know these truths . . .

4 WE MUST INDIVIDUALLY **RECEIVE** JESUS CHRIST AS SAVIOR AND LORD; THEN WE CAN KNOW GOD PERSONALLY AND EXPERIENCE HIS LOVE.

We Must Receive Christ

"But as many as received Him, to them He gave the right to become children of God, even to those who believe in His name" (John 1:12).

We Receive Christ Through Faith

"For by grace you have been saved through faith; and that not of yourselves, it is the gift of God; not as a result of works, that no one should boast" (Ephesians 2:8,9).

When We Receive Christ, We Experience a New Birth. (Read John 3:1-8.)

We Receive Christ by Personal Invitation

(Christ is speaking): "Behold, I stand at the door and knock; if anyone hears My voice and opens the door, I will come in to him" (Revelation 3:20).

Receiving Christ involves turning to God from self (repentance) and trusting Christ to come into our lives to forgive our sins and to make us the kind of people He wants us to be. Just to agree intellectually that Jesus Christ is the Son of God and that He died on the cross for our sins is not enough. Nor is it enough to have an emotional experience. We receive Jesus Christ by faith, as an act of the will.

These two circles represent two kinds of lives:

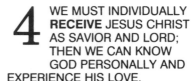

SELF-DIRECTED LIFE
S – Self is on the throne
† – Christ is out-side the life
● – Interests are directed by self, often resulting in discord and frustration

CHRIST-DIRECTED LIFE
† – Christ is in the life and on the throne
S – Self is yielding to Christ
● – Interests are directed by Christ, resulting in harmony with God's plan

Which circle best represents your life? Which circle would you like to have represent your life?

The following explains how you can invite Jesus Christ into your life:

YOU CAN RECEIVE CHRIST RIGHT NOW BY FAITH THROUGH PRAYER

(Prayer is talking with God)

God knows your heart and is not so concerned with your words as He is with the attitude of your heart. The following is a suggested prayer:

"Lord Jesus, I want to know You personally. Thank You for dying on the cross for my sins. I open the door of my life and receive You as my Savior and Lord. Thank You for forgiving my sins and giving me eternal life. Take control of the throne of my life. Make me the kind of person You want me to be."

Does this prayer express the desire of your heart?

If it does, pray this prayer right now, and Christ will come into your life, as He promised.

How to Know That Christ Is in Your Life

Did you receive Christ into your life? According to His promise in Revelation 3:20, where is Christ right now in relation to you? Christ said that He would come into your life and be your friend so you can know Him personally. Would He mislead you? On what authority do you know that God has answered your prayer? (The trustworthiness of God Himself and His Word.)

The Bible Promises Eternal Life to All Who Receive Christ

"And the witness is this, that God has given us eternal life, and this life is in His Son. He who has the Son has the life; he who does not have the Son of God does not have the life. These things I have written to you who believe in the name of the Son of God, in order that you may know that you have eternal life" (1 John 5:11-13).

Thank God often that Christ is in your life and that He will never leave you (Hebrews 13:5). You can know on the basis of His promise that Christ lives in you and that you have eternal life, from the very moment you invite Him in. He will not deceive you.

An important reminder . . .

DO NOT DEPEND ON FEELINGS

The promise of God's Word, the Bible — not our feelings — is our authority. The Christian lives by faith (trust) in the trustworthiness of God Himself and His Word. This train diagram illustrates the relationship between fact (God and His Word), faith (our trust in God and His Word), and feeling (the result of our faith and obedience) (John 14:21).

The train will run with or without the caboose. However, it would be useless to attempt to pull the train by the caboose. In the same way, we, as Christians, do not depend on feelings or emotions, but we place our faith (trust) in the trustworthiness of God and the promises of His Word.

Fellowship in a Good Church

God's Word admonishes us not to forsake "the assembling of ourselves together" (Hebrews 10:25). Several logs burn brightly together, but put one aside on the cold hearth and the fire goes out. So it is with your relationship with other Christians. If you do not belong to a church, do not wait to be invited. Take the initiative; call the pastor of a nearby church where Christ is honored and His Word is preached. Start this week, and make plans to attend regularly.

Suggestions for Christian Growth

Spiritual growth results from trusting Jesus Christ. "The righteous man shall live by faith" (Galatians 3:11). A life of faith will enable you to trust God increasingly with every detail of your life.

* * * * *

Notes

Chapter 1

1. Quoted in *Evidence That Demands A Verdict*, Josh McDowell (San Bernardino, CA: Here's Life Publishers, 1972), p. 350.

Chapter 2

1. As quoted by Alvin Plantinga in "Reason and Belief in God," *The Intellectuals Speak Out About God* (Chicago: Regnery Gateway, 1984), p. 186. Used by permission.

2. Frank Morison, *Who Moved The Stone?* (London: Faber and Faber, 1959), p. 11. Used by permission of Zondervan Publishing House.

3. Quoted in *Ten Basic Steps for Christian Maturity* (San Bernardino, CA: Here's Life Publishers, 1982), p. 233.

Chapter 3

1. C. S. Lewis, *Mere Christianity* (New York: Macmillan, 1952), pp. 55-56. Used by permission.

Chapter 4

1. C. S. Lewis, *Mere Christianity* (New York: Macmillan, 1952), p. 111. Used by permission.

2. Francis Schaeffer, *The God Who Is There* (Downers Grove, IL: Inter-Varsity Press, 1968), p. 133.

Chapter 5

1. Charles Swindoll, *Come Before Winter* (Portland, OR: Multnomah Press, 1985), p. 89.

2. Jerry Bridges, *The Pursuit of Holiness* (Colorado Springs, CO: NavPress, 1978), p. 31. Used by permission.

3. O. Quentin Hyder, M.D., *The Christian's Handbook of Psychiatry* (Old Tappan, NJ: Revell, 1971), p. 121.

4. Larry Richards, *Born To Grow* (Wheaton, IL: Victor, 1974), p. 39. Used by permission.

Chapter 6

1. Alex Haley, *Roots* (Garden City: Doubleday, 1976), p. 664. Used by permission.

2. E. M. Blaiklock as quoted in *Evidence That Demands A Verdict*, Josh McDowell (San Bernardino, CA: Here's Life Publishers, 1972), p. 75.

3. As quoted in *Evidence That Demands a Verdict,* p. 68.

4. Paul Little, *Know Why You Believe* (Downers Grove, IL: InterVarsity Press, 1968), p. 34.

Chapter 7

1. O. Hallesby, *Prayer* (Minneapolis: Augsburg, 1959), p. 119. Used by permission.

Chapter 8

1. Bill Bright, "Have You Made The Wonderful Discovery Of The Spirit-filled Life?" (San Bernardino, CA: Campus Crusade For Christ, 1966), p. 12.

Chapter 10

1. Tim LaHaye, *How to Study the Bible for Yourself* (Irvine, CA: Harvest House, 1976), p. 128. Used by permission.

2. Francis Cosgrove, Jr., *Essentials of New Life* (Colorado Springs, CO: NavPress, 1978), pp. 68-69. Used by permission.

Chapter 11

1. Charles Colson, *Born Again* (Old Tappen, NJ: Chosen Books, 1976), p. 139.

2. Colson, *Born Again,* p. 308.

3. Gene Getz, *The Measure of a Church* (Glendale, CA: Regal Books, 1975), p. 33.

Chapter 12

1. J. Dwight Pentecost, *The Joy of Living* (Grand Rapids, MI: Zondervan, 1973), p. 137.

2. Samuel Clemens, *Great Short Works of Mark Twain* (New York: Harper & Row, 1967), p. 18. Used by permission.